THE GOLDEN TORTOISE

ALSO BY EDWARD TICK

Sacred Mountain: Encounters with the Viet Nam Beast (1989)

The Practice of Dream Healing: Bringing Ancient Greek Mysteries into Modern Medicine (2001)

War and the Soul (2005)

THE GOLDEN TORTOISE

Journeys in Viet Nam

―∞―

BY EDWARD TICK

Red Hen Press 🐔 Los Angeles

The Golden Tortoise

Cover image: *Dien Bien–A History–A Poem* by Pham May. Black and white painting© 2005 by Pham May

Book design by Michael Vukadinovich
Cover Design by Mark E. Cull

ISBN: 1-59709-008-5

Library of Congress Catalog Card Number: 2004117568

Published by Red Hen Press

The City of Los Angeles Cultural Affairs Department, California Arts Council, Los Angeles County Arts Commission and the National Endowment for the Arts partially support Red Hen Press.

First Edition

Acknowledgements

My war haiku in Part I first appeared in *On Sacred Mountain: Vietnam Remembered*, Battle Ground, IN: High/Coo Press, 1984. They reappeared in the narrative of my first five years of work with veterans in *Sacred Mountain: Encounters with the Vietnam Beast*, Santa Fe: NM, Moon Bear Press, 1989.

"Long-Haired Warrior" in Part VI first appeared in *Simply Haiku*, Spring 2005, 3:1.

The translation of Do Trung Quan's poem "Que Huong" in Part VI is by Tran Dinh Song and Edward Tick. Que huong is pronounced "quay hung."

The book's epigram is from *Lessons in Emptiness* by Tran Thai Tong, translated by Thich Nhat Hanh and published in *Zen Keys*, New York: Doubleday Anchor, 1995, p. 182. The reference to Tong's teaching in Part VI is from *Zen Keys*, p. 170.

W.D. Ehrhart's excerpt in Part VI is from "Making the Children Behave," *To Those Who Have Gone Home Tired*, New York: Thunder's Mouth Press, 1984, p. 20. It also appears in his early account of returning to Viet Nam, *Going Back: A Poet Who Was Once a Marine Returns to Vietnam*, Wallingford, PA: Pendle Hill Publications, 1987, p. 4.

The excerpts from *Ca Dao* in Part IV and from Nguyen Du's "Call to Wandering Souls" in Part VI are taken from Huu Ngoc, *Sketches for a Portrait of Vietnamese Culture*, Ha Noi: Gioi Publishers, 1998, pp. 632-4 and 881. The translation is Dr. Huu's.

The poem by a survivor of the Vinh Moc tunnels quoted in Part VI appears in the Vinh Moc Museum beneath a war-era black and white photo of a toddler in the dark tunnels clutching a rifle. No attribution is given.

I express my deep appreciation to the editors, writers and translators of all the above works. In addition, for their invaluable contributions to this work, I express great gratitude to:

Steven Leibo, Prof. of International History and Politics, and Chair of International Studies at The Sage Colleges. Steven was my co-leader on my first four journeys. I am also grateful for his co-creating and team-teaching our course "The Viet Nam Experience" at Sage. Our course began as an historical and psychological survey of the war; Viet Nam itself taught us to broaden it to the full experience of that country. Finally, I express yet more gratitude to Steven for co-founding and co-directing our study and teaching center, The Sage Center on Violence and Healing.

Tran Dinh Song. Good, intelligent, generous, sweet, wise, learned, patient, kind, Song has been our in-country guide for every journey. He has taught our groups uncountable gems about Vietnamese history and culture and advises on all aspects of travel from matters daily to historical and spiritual. I proudly consider Song our third co-leader of these journeys and I call him my *ngu'o'i ban giao vien*, my teacher-friend.

Marcia Silva and Richard Schonberger of Global Spectrum, Marcia's agency specializing in travel adventures to Viet Nam and Southeast Asia. Marcia and Dick have been generous, patient, helpful and knowledgeable in every aspect of planning, developing, shaping and conducting our journeys and philanthropic activities in Viet Nam.

Dr. Huu Ngoc. Dr. Huu shares his scholarship and hospitality every time we visit Ha Noi. His comprehensive book *Sketches for a Portrait of Vietnamese Culture,* noted above, a collection of essays on every aspect of Vietnamese history, culture, mythology, and literature, is an indispensable resource. I deeply acknowledge Dr. Ngoc and his book's influence on my understanding and writing about Viet Nam.

Deena Metzger, wise elder, writer, mentor, "pal," who greeted Turtle immediately and served as the angel introducing this book to Red Hen Press.

All our travelers—veterans, their relatives and survivors, teachers, activists, protestors, students, adventurers, vacationers. These trips would be nothing without them and their generous trust, support, desire to learn, teach, heal, and pass the lessons of war and peace on to the next generation.

All my veteran patients, colleagues and friends over the last quarter century. Their trust and urgency to heal and preserve their stories have been among the great teachers and treasures of my life.

I especially acknowledge my early war and writing mentor William Herrick, veteran of the Lincoln Brigade in the Spanish Civil War, and Jim Lantz, medic in Viet Nam who awarded me his patch, both of whom died while I was completing this book, and Preston Stern, grunt and resister in the war, whose tenth anniversary of death coincides with this publication. I write for you all.

The Vietnamese people. When at war, they are at war. When at peace, they truly are at peace. They are eternally and infinitely kind, forgiving, welcoming, hospitable, and wise. We Americans are frightened and angry; they are not. They help us heal; may we help them rebuild and thus create peace. I especially acknowledge and thank my dear *chau*, my "nephews" Vuong Toan Nam and Do Thanh Son who have helped me learn new depths of love, wisdom, humility and right values.

My wife Kate Dahlstedt and our children Jeremy, Gabriel and Sappho. I would not be who I am or able to orchestrate and guide these journeys without the support, generosity, understanding and willing sacrifice of my family. They provide all that a traveler needs in order to know that wherever he goes he is home and that his true home always travels with him.

For your gifts

Turtle

I make this offering

If the war is ended and no one dreams of vengeance
What need is there of taking the sword from its sheath?

—Emperor Tran Thai Tong, 13th century

Contents

POETRY, PILGRIMAGE, AND HEALING FROM WAR

I did not go to Viet Nam during the war. Instead, I protested it with all my youthful passion. In 1979, a mere four years after the war's end and while still a young man, I began working as a psychotherapist with combat and non-combat veterans.

In the cauldron of the mind, the horrors of war can boil and rage for a lifetime. In the intimacy and privacy of the healing relationship, those horrors are invited to parade in full panoply before a single witness. It was there that I served, there that I went to war. During a quarter century of work with veterans, first of Viet Nam and later of World War II, Korea, El Salvador, Lebanon, the first Gulf and present Iraqi Wars, Northern Ireland, and survivors of Nazi and Serbian concentration camps, war's ghoulish spirit came alive in my mind, heart and imagination. Even to those of us who were not in the combat zone, war's imagery burns like psychic napalm, frying its way through layers of psyche and culture to hit the soul. War and its legacy disturbed my life so much that its healing became a primary calling.

Through hundreds of veteran clients and thousands of therapy hours, I became intimate with the Viet Nam War and the ravaged country of Viet Nam. It became inevitable that I would need to travel to Viet Nam myself. I needed to complete a journey begun long ago as both protestor and healer on the home front. I needed to make the country and people of Viet Nam my own too, to formulate my personal answer to the questions people inevitably ask in America, "Were you in Viet Nam?" or in southeast Asia, "Were you here before '75?" I needed to learn first hand about this people and land we married forever through our war with them. From my accumulated years with veterans, I carried more war stories than any score of them together. Like a veteran, I needed to replace my own war imagery with new mental pictures of healing from the Viet Nam that lives on.

In May and June 2000, just weeks after the 25th anniversary of the end of the war, Prof. Steven Leibo, Chair of International Studies at The Sage Colleges, and I co-led our first journey of education and reconciliation to Viet Nam. Now, annually, I escort groups of veterans, vets' wives, siblings and children, Amerasian young adults, professors and teachers, protestors, activists, adventurers and students throughout contemporary Viet Nam. We visit old battlefields, Buddhist shrines, cemeteries, schools and healing centers. We travel through large cities and remote villages, museums of art, war, and culture in both the south and north. We meet with

Vietnamese veterans who fought Japanese, French, Chinese, and Khmer Rouge Cambodians as well as Americans. We seek to encounter the Vietnamese people and culture as they are, to discover what they feel about war and about us. We seek to discover what has become of them since what they call the American War ended. We seek to build a personal and lasting reconciliation, peace, and friendship within ourselves and between our people and countries that were once, wrongly and tragically, enemies.

The Golden Tortoise takes you through Viet Nam today. We visit its sites to replace images of suffering with images of healing from the contemporary people and landscape, replicating the way such images are replaced in the minds of contemporary veteran and civilian travelers. It explores the land, culture, people, history, spirituality and mythology of Viet Nam. It demonstrates how immersion in this land and culture can bring healing and transformation to those still suffering the inner ravages of war. And it records the fascinating, rapid, hopeful and troubling changes now taking place in Viet Nam as it heals its war legacy and struggles with the transition from a society that was isolated, closed, controlled, rural, agrarian and tradition-bound toward one that is open and becoming world market, consumer and technology-driven. These changes, says Ha Noi scholar and writer Dr. Huu Ngoc, represent "Viet Nam's most difficult war, a war to save our soul, a war in our heads." *The Golden Tortoise* demonstrates the possibilities of transforming and ending the "war in our heads" for Vietnamese and Americans alike.

The guiding image of my earlier prose and poetry collections on the war in Viet Nam was the Sacred Mountain, or *Nui Than* in Vietnamese. This image literally refers to several mountains in Viet Nam that have been places of pilgrimage and worship and of terrible combat. One of many is Marble Mountain, famous as Buddhist shrine, Viet Cong field hospital, and site of two terrible battles. Another is *Nui Ba Den*, Lady Black Mountain, west of Ho Chi Minh City near the Cambodian Border. We visit both herein.

It was on Nui Ba Den that my first combat veteran patient experienced these events, recorded in *On Sacred Mountain*, my first small collection of war haiku. That collection was, in part, constructed of imagery and experiences passed on to me by my veteran therapy patients.

> Fire leaps from a tree
> the only safe place to hide
> behind a body

⸻

Outside the cavern
the screams of my dying friend
I clean my rifle

⸻

The chopper lands—
ten men sprint, heads down—
I board alone

I ascended that mountain with veterans who fought there. I explored those caves. I prayed and lit incense for all the war dead, and for the healing of the living, in the Buddhist temple atop the mountain. Today, Nui Ba Den is green and peaceful. During my first visit, I was welcomed to the temple by an old woman with a beatific smile. A young boy guided me to all the divine images adorning the temple. During my second visit, I guided an American veteran in prayers for the soul of a 14-year-old boy he had killed in a firefight 35 years before and just a few miles away. And my third visit occurred on the day of my 19th wedding anniversary. The resident abbot chanted blessings over my wife Kate and me as we offered incense at his altar. Each visit, I was overjoyed that this image from my first collection is still accurate:

On Sacred Mountain
flames in the temple,
the monk's mantra

Today the burning flames are no longer the flames of tracers and bombs, but only of incense and candles, grief and forgiveness.

Beyond the concrete, the Sacred Mountain is a spiritual guidepost for healing the wounds of war. One veteran, Preston Stern, used to pray to Nui Ba Den from Long Binh Jail, where he was incarcerated for refusing to fight after his squad was decimated by friendly fire and he was sure the war was evil. The mountain steadied his soul when everything around him, including our side, was hostile. He had desperately wanted to return, climb the mountain's slopes, and fast and pray on its summit. He died of Agent Orange-related liver disease in 1995. I traveled for him, and so many others.

Nui Than, explains my friend and in-country guide Tran Dinh Song, himself a veteran as well as a teacher of literature and language, is a universal image in Viet Nam as well as other traditional cultures worldwide. It is an archetype of the spirit instantly recognized by all Vietnamese people from peasant to scholar. Sacred Mountain is Nui Ba Den and all the other mountains on which many of us, Americans and Vietnamese alike, fought and died or cried and prayed. Sacred Mountain is the composite of those mountains that are growing green again, where we can now travel in safety in order to seek healing and reconciliation. Sacred Mountain is the place of eternal renewal where what was most horrible can be washed clean with the return of life. Sacred Mountain is a place where understanding and forgiveness are possible when we have the courage to embrace our former enemies as friends. That is what we find offered everywhere in Viet Nam today. Sacred Mountain is the place our souls seek that truly and eternally reminds and teaches us of what is most precious, most important, and should never be profaned.

Poetry and the Healing Journey

Why, in my first chapbook *On Sacred Mountain*, did I use such a delicate form as haiku to express something as brutal as war? And why do I continue to utilize English language haiku, haiku series, and haibun, such as are found in this collection, in addition to Western styles, as primary forms for exploring war's legacy and healing?

As a poetic form, haiku appears to be spontaneous, fragmentary, non-conceptual, imagistic and immediate, like the experience of war itself. Further, as haikuist and critic Ikuyo Yokimura of Gifu Women's University in Japan has observed, haiku and war share a natural link in that haiku is fundamentally nature poetry while war is fundamentally the destruction of nature.

Since haiku explores the human encounter with raw nature, war haiku explores the destructive dimensions of this encounter in several simultaneous ways. It exposes the darkest dimensions of our human nature. It offers painful examples of what we do to nature. And it poetically replicates a war-like experience for the reader.

Yet haiku, like all poetry, like nature itself, is ultimately creative and life affirming. Thus, haiku can also be a vehicle for expressing war's lessons. And in our devotion to healing, poetry in general and haiku specifically can help us to psychically and imagistically reconstitute those fragments of world, mind, and soul that were severed by war and violence.

In Viet Nam more obviously than in America, reminders of war are found everywhere. Every generation, including those still being born, carry its wounds. But in Viet Nam war wounds are not necessarily the deadly psychic wounds that have caused too many Americans to hide, collapse, cease functioning or living. Rather, in large part, the Vietnamese people and culture embrace their wounds as honorable scars, surrounding them with spiritual and practical wisdom and loving communal support, enabling the people and land to endure and thrive. Thus, pilgrimage to the Viet Nam of today and re-creation and contemplation of that pilgrimage through poetry can help heal what we once brutalized. And by pilgrimage I mean what serious travelers from every epoch and tradition have meant. We undertake pilgrimage to distant and mysterious places in order to awaken, educate, heal and deepen our souls.

The Golden Tortoise is in haibun form. Haibun is brief prose travel narrative interspersed at key moments with haiku. It is a traditional Japanese form of travelogue perfected, for example, by haiku masters Basho in numerous travel sketches including his masterpiece *The Narrow Road to the Deep North* (1694) and by Issa in *The Year of My Life* (1819). As an old Asian form of travel writing, it is ideally suited as a report on pilgrimage where we journey many tedious miles for those moments of awareness and encounter that awaken and revivify the soul.

One principle way we learn, experience and embody another culture is through its language. As we learn a culture's language we experience its thought-world.

Vietnamese is a tonal language; to our ears it sounds almost chanted. All its words are pronounced with one of six different tones. The same sound pronounced differently will have a different meaning. For example, *ma* can mean "ghost," "young rice," or "however," depending on pronunciation. Further, Vietnamese is monosyllabic. Its written words consist of one syllable and their proper spelling expresses this. Thus, the correct spelling of the country is not Vietnam, as commonly appears in English. Rather, it is Viet Nam, meaning Country of the Southern Viets. The proper spelling of its capital is not Hanoi but Ha Noi, meaning City Amidst the Waters. Some place names derive from ethnic minority languages other than Viet. Sometimes they are spelled as one word, like Pleiku, sometimes as more, as in Sai Gon.

For individuals and nations alike, what we do not know or understand about other people or cultures allows us to project our fantasies, wishes, fears, judgments, and demons onto them. We began military involvement against Viet Nam before we knew anything about their country or culture. In fact, there was no book in English on Viet Nam until 1958. But to achieve peace, we must find out who the other people are, then transform them from enemies back to interesting people with whom we share an important history. Finally we must become friends.

When seeking friends and allies, when involving ourselves with other countries, cultures, and peoples, and when immersing in another culture in search of healing and peacemaking, it is critical that we learn, respect and practice all that we can about that culture's language, values, beliefs, customs and traditions. We must meet, greet and treat them on their own terms and in ways that signal respect, empathy and integrity.

As much as is possible and comfortable, I have used the proper Vietnamese spelling for terms or names of people and natural and civic, religious and historical sites. Though unfamiliar to our eyes, this will increase the reader's experience of immersion in Viet Nam and its culture. It will also, in its small way, help correct basic misrepresentations of Viet Nam in American eyes.

Reconciling our pained history with Viet Nam must be a Western as well as Eastern, American as well as Vietnamese journey. Thus the poetic chronicle of our first journey, Return to Sacred Mountain, constitutes Part II of this collection. Since returning to the Sacred Mountain in 2000, Prof. Leibo and I continue to lead regular pilgrimages to Viet Nam. Our journeys of 2001, 2002, and 2004 are chronicled in Parts III: Floating Upriver, IV: Ice Moon Setting, and VI: River of Peace. These sections continue the haibun travel narrative but include structured or free verse lyrics more familiar to modern readers as well as haiku individually and in series, and tanka, an earlier elegant Japanese 5-line form. And this pilgrimage that began in America with sustained efforts to heal from our war finds additional fulfillment not only in the land of Viet Nam but in its history, mythology, and spirit. Part V, The Legend of King Le Loi, retells a foundational Vietnamese myth in epic verse.

King Le Loi was both a mythic and historical figure. In the fifteenth century he led the rebellion that was ultimately successful in ousting the Ming Chinese after a brutal twenty-year occupation. The cruelty of this occupation and the spirit of Le Loi's rebellion at once recall the earlier 1,200 years of Chinese domination and in mysterious ways predict Viet Nam's difficult yet ultimately successful struggle to regain its independence from all foreign invaders, including us.

After Le Loi's rebellion was successful and Vietnamese independence re-established, a golden tortoise, *Kim Quay* in Vietnamese, retrieved the magic sword that was a divine aid only loaned to humanity by the Emperor of Waters. The retrieval of the sword by the turtle, serving as a celestial messenger, signaled the end of war and beginning of a new era of peace, independence, cooperation, prosperity, longevity and legitimacy. Hence the title of this collection *The Golden Tortoise*, for Viet Nam has its independence and is experiencing rebirth. And we Americans are invited into a new era of peace and friendship, reconciliation and mutual healing with Viet Nam. Poetry derived from both cultures' interpenetrating experiences can further such an evolution.

Le Loi's voice tells his story, yet it is also our story. Le Loi reflects on all he and we have learned about the call to service, hatred of violence, necessity of sacrifice, and toil and impulses toward wise and peaceful self-rule. Perhaps allowing Le Loi to speak in the epic voice will unite his Vietnamese myth with heroic tales the world over, helping remind us of the meaning of honor, devotion, sacrifice and, that concept so dearly loved by Vietnamese and Americans alike, freedom.

RETURN TO SACRED MOUNTAIN

2000

I: Viet Nam

I travel through Viet Nam to report from the war front, 25 years later.

> Weary ghost
> wandering
> young rice sprouts

—∞—

I arrive in Ho Chi Minh City, the old Sai Gon. A late afternoon monsoon pours tubs from the sky. As street vendors dart for cover, I take silent refuge with a retired American air force commander in the small lobby of a colonial-era hotel.

> Gray haired veteran
> sitting behind his blue pane
> dribbling warm rain

—∞—

After strolling among the early morning hoards along the Sai Gon river, I take the road west out of the city. I pass through verdant rice fields and villages rolling toward the Cu Chi Tunnel complex. I stop for water in this thronging countryside where the local people say that during the war they had more bombs than rice:

> Smiling grandmother
> leaning on her metal crutch
> offering pink flowers

—∞—

I stoop and squeeze through the Cu Chi Tunnels. Here guerillas and peasants lived in and fought from underground villages, often for years at a time, during both the French and American wars:

Bombs showering rice—
kindergarten, hospitals
safe beneath our earth

I travel through Trang Bang, once saturated with war. I drive along flat, dusty Highway 32, where a reporter snapped the photo that showed the world Kim Phuc, one napalmed little girl running naked from her anguish.

A soccer ball bounces
by the flooded rice paddy—
the echo of her scream

Nui Ba Den means Lady Black Mountain. Here, long ago, Lady Black jumped to her death rather than marry a false love. Monks have prayed to her spirit ever since.

During the war, this mountain was the scene of boulder-to-boulder slaughter. Now it is the rocky perch of a Buddhist temple:

Flames in the temple-
my burning incense,
my guide-boy's twinkle

The resident monk strikes his gong. A former war protestor, I pray with a combat veteran on the temple's high stone portico:

"Hell no, we won't go"—
"The night belongs to Charlie"—
together before Buddha

We gaze toward the nearby mountains of the Cambodian border and tell stories.

Glassy, vacant stare—
toasting friends dead on this rock
our eyes melt to tears

———

On the rocky slopes, I seek the cave where my friend had been trapped:

Where he hid behind
friends' fallen bodies,
look —red dragonflies

———

Descending the mountain, I look back and bow:

Gray rocks, green trees
climbing Lady Black's grave—
the spine of Buddha

———

Back in Ho Chi Minh City, I visit the War Remnants Museum. Formerly called the Museum of American War Atrocities, its name and exhibits have been softened to ease our pain.

Smiling, bright-eyed boy,
bloated fetus with two heads—
face to face

———

I arrive in dusty Pleiku in the Central Highlands. Only a village before the war, it grew into this busy market city as an American stronghold. As I step off the bus, an old veteran of the South Vietnamese army greets me:

Ranger's cap, toothless grin—
selling news from a rusty bike—
"Where have you been, my friends?"

———❀———

A former American combat engineer, who once hunted mines buried in the dirt roads of these mountains, wanders the crowded Pleiku market:

> Sniper? Mortar? Booby trap?
> In a straw hat, yellow shirt
> he buys a Highlands basket

———❀———

My traveling companions and I deliver the gift of a water buffalo to a Montengaard village. The native people thank us with a gong music ceremony, their shy young women weaving a dance of friendship. I spend the night in their longhouse, where I dream of their moon goddess:

> Red coals, white fireflies,
> the echo of village gongs—
> glimpsing her black eyes

———❀———

In a tiny crossroads village market, I mispronounce the tone of Vietnamese words, which changes their meanings:

> Smell of sweet biscuits;
> sun on blue sarongs;
> "Friend, where are you from?"
> "I am a noodle."

———❀———

Off Highway 1 in the central highlands outside the village of An Khe, we help an American veteran search for his old firebase:

> Patrolling the red clay road
> snaking between green hills,
> breathing easily

— ◈ —

The vet locates his former station, first dismayed, then joyous at the little he finds there.

> In the red mud
> stretching to his old firebase
> bike tracks, hoof prints

— ◈ —

I step off my bus in a small coastal plains village to pray in front of a military cemetery for a veteran friend from home near his old air base:

> Stones at attention
> wriggling in the noon heat —
> yellow dragonfly

— ◈ —

Off a beach south of My Lai, I frolic in the waves with village children the evening before my visit to the Memorial where we killed many just like these.

> How close they are
> as the sea swallows the sun:
> the laugh, the scream

— ◈ —

Early the next morning, I travel the trafficked road to My Lai:

> A hundred bicycles
> in the dawn-stained dust
> two old veterans

— ◈ —

In My Lai, among the house mounds and memorial tablets to the dead, where a 75 year old survivor of the massacre tends the gardens:

> Before the tomb
> burning incense
> with no innocence

—⁂—

> Arm in arm
> over the dead
> arm in arm

—⁂—

I continue north to climb the winding stairways of Marble Mountain, pockmarked with shell holes and temple caves:

> Glittering marble,
> dripping sweat drops,
> unmoving Buddha

—⁂—

Outside Da Nang, I light incense before the giant white statue of Buddha. Though located in a hotly contested area, it remained unscathed during the entire war:

> Bombs, bullets, blood—
> snails nesting on his scalp—
> he sits, stares, smiles

—⁂—

In the coastal town of Hoi An, I visit with a young marble sculptor, Do Thanh Son, in his closet-sized shop.

> Carving tools, stone gods
> crowded in dusty corners
> he reads Spinoza

———⚭———

I visit the scarred palaces and charred walls of the citadel of Hue, old imperial capital and scene of our war's most gruesome battle. I light incense to the dead in its ruins. Then at night I wander the local streets:

> The armless boy
> with his begging bowl, smiling,
> "How are you?"

———⚭———

Lights dance on the famous river flowing from distant sites of brutal combat down through crowded villages and then through the center of Hue.

> On Hamburger Hill
> flowers carpet the swift river
> that flows in Perfume

———⚭———

I travel Quang Tri Province, near the old DMZ, scene of brutal fighting and atrocities . . .

> You torched my son.
> His soul wanders forever.
> I will not see yours.

———⚭———

and defoliation . . .

> Green rice paddies
> surrounding weedy bomb craters—
> ghost of a jungle

———⚭———

where unexploded shells still maim and kill:

Black ants cleaning
a buffalo carcass—
peasants hunting mines

—❧—

Deep in the mountains, I visit a minority village perched along the old Ho Chi Minh Trail. I am invited into the chief's hut built, in part, from old war materiel.

Coffee beans and grandson
roasting in the noon sun
on rusting chopper blades

—❧—

Later I visit the huge Trung Son Cemetery, by itself in the green country-side, interring over 100,000 of those killed while serving on the Ho Chi Minh Trail.

Dusk cloaks the war bridge
and ten thousand grave stones—
children chew my gum

—❧—

Nearby, another American veteran searches for his old station. He meets Viet Cong and North Vietnamese Army veterans at the overgrown site that was his firebase.

Red dusk, broken tarmac—
the enemy approaches
to shake hands

—❧—

I finally reach Ha Noi, the North Vietnamese capital, to walk the tree and vendor choked sidewalks we had learned to dread. Ha Noi's people are proud of their unified country.

> Crossing the street
> thick with bikes, cyclos, vendors—
> one among One

Ha Noi is built around the Lake of the Sword Restoration. There a golden tortoise, the God of Heaven's messenger, promised to help an early king achieve independence if the king did not abuse his power.

> The thick mist lifts
> from the old battlefield—
> tortoise in the lake

I travel east to Ha Long Bay, on the coast of the South China Sea:

> The gray buffalo
> munches green grass.
> The gray sea
> creeps toward the rice.

Between Ha Long and Ha Noi, I visit Rosy Jade Humanity Center, a school and home for hundreds of children with Agent Orange disabilities.

> Twisted claws
> embroidering
> young rice

It is rice harvest time in the north:

The farmer's back bends
beneath bobbing rice sheaves.
Mist envelops me.

———

Returning to Ha Noi, I visit the Temple of Literature, Viet Nam's first university, 1,000 years old.

Red flowers bedeck
the gray hall of sages —
a war cripple begs

———

There I struggle to grasp the Vietnamese Buddha's gift to these people that helped them endure and triumph —the joyful embrace of all that life offers, including its sorrow.

The war cripple begs
before the sages' gray hall —
yet look —red blossoms

———

II: Thailand

Like so many GIs during the war, I retreat to Thailand for "R&R." I find lodgings in a simple guesthouse perched above a dirty river in Ayuthea, the medieval capital of Siam, one hour north of Bangkok. There I meditate on my journey, on war and the human condition.

> Teak wood porch
> rotting above the current,
> empty chair rocking

Ayuthea is studded with Buddhist temples called *wats*. I explore numerous *wats*, both ancient and in use, sparkling and eroding.

> Red dragonflies buzz
> crumbling stone Buddhas
> in gold silk robes

> The golden Buddha
> stares at the steady current
> of the muddy river.
> Boats, branches, debris float by.

> Buddha's half torso
> steadfast in the noon swelter —
> sweet burning incense

I wander back streets of the dirty, crowded village.

> Bucket of turtles
> in the sweltering market—
> the toothless vendor grins

———✸———

Staring at this slow-flowing Thai river reminds me of My Lai.

> Village water ditch—
> the dead stretch their arms to me—
> hum of dragonflies

———✸———

It is my last night in Southeast Asia. I sit under the full moon that is also the Vietnamese goddess of beauty, and prepare to return home:

> A cloak of moonlight
> hangs from her velvet shoulders—
> footprints on the sea

III: FLOATING UPRIVER

2001

One year later, I return to Viet Nam to further explore how war affected the Vietnamese people and land, how they carry it, and how to help our vets. I travel through Tay Ninh Province, fiercely bombed and burned during the war. I revisit the mountain sacred to all Vietnamese, once the scene of myths and battles, now of prayer and frolic for both Vietnamese and travelers.

Lady Black Mountain

For endless years
the afternoon clouds
on the mountain's summit
were a virgin's burial shroud.
Now she wears a white garland
and wind chimes ring.

———

In Ho Chi Minh City, I become friends with a 13-year old street girl. Tuyen, the sole support of her mother and baby sister, is one of the seemingly infinite number of street vendors —children, the elderly, the disabled—hawking postcards and books to tourists. She attends school during the day then must remain on the streets late into the night—for as long as it takes to earn one dollar.

Tuyen

Crying our wares
in the midnight shadows —
the painted woman and me

selling postcards—
the way I grow rice
for my family

don't be offended
by the whore's anger—
she too must eat

your people come
for war, shopping, movies—
I am always here

why is street life
so hard? not enough time
to read

who dares say
that noon is more beautiful
than midnight?

———⊗⊗⊗———

I travel south to explore the labyrinthine waterways and stilt-supported huts of the Mekong Delta. I seek to answer the urgent appeal of an American veteran, a former river rat who cruised the delta on swift, armed patrol boats. "When I arrived on the Mekong in '65, it was a fertile wonderland. By the time I left one year later, Agent Orange had turned it into a wasted moonscape. Please, I must know. Is life returning to the delta?"

Green

The Mekong Delta is green. The palms lining its shore are green. The tall grasses are green. Its floating clumps of water lilies are broad-leafed green. The water itself is muddy green. The air, damp, thick, humid, and heavy, smells green. And even the gray clouds blanketing the sky seem tinged with reflected green.

The steel barrels floating in the water are green—some painted green, others rusty steel reflecting green. And the hundreds of poor, simple, unpainted houses and fishing sampans are green. Their wood is stained and tempered by water, rain, breeze, and sweat until it has turned dark green.

Along the river banks, where there are no houses, the jungle or bush fades away in layer upon layer of floating green, ankle deep, knee high, chest high, mottled levels of green, until the brush finally becomes impenetrable in dark depths of green.

But the children's eyes are black. And their shining smiles and waving hands and blown kisses save us from drowning in endless swells of green.

———

I stay with a local family in their house perched on stilts and mud. I sit on their porch above the eternally flowing waters through nights so deep it seems like only sounds, not sights, exist. With the roosters I greet the awakening sun.

Water Lillies

Palm fronds rise above thick green brush—
prayer banners of the scattered thatched roofs.
Chickens cluck. Unseen children sing.
On our stilt porch a gaggle of men
surround their cracked warm teapot
while on the olive river below
an old woman in petal pink
rows as she hawks her dawn-picked greens.

These water lily clumps—broad leaves, tangled stems—
floated downstream in the evening.
As the sun's globe cracks the white haze—
an egg breaking its celestial shell—
I sit above the mud bank
and watch them float upriver again,
as far from the cool northern cascades
as they are from the sea that breathes them.

———

I travel with an American veteran who was an infantry grunt stationed in the countryside jungles north of the old Sai Gon. For decades he has been haunted by the ghosts of men, boys and a village he helped destroy.

A Veteran's Return

His first day in the new Viet Nam, he stands before a statue of Ho Chi Minh in the city renamed for him:

> The sandaled feet
> of Uncle Ho's statue—
> dripping tears

It is our Memorial Day. Before leaving the city, we stop to pray at a Buddhist temple thick with icons of mythological and religious figures.

> Palms hot with gun heat
> he raises burning incense
> to the dragon's mouth

As we travel through the countryside, he stares speechlessly at the prairie of rice paddies. Spirits seem to answer his incense offering:

> Dark waters
> emerald rice shoots
> slogging ghosts

We arrive at the Cao Dai Temple near Tay Ninh. The last one to climb off our bus, his face twists with old pain he can no longer bury:

> Crying for the dead
> in the temple's cool shadow
> he calls home

We search old maps to locate his former jungle base. We travel bumpy dirt roads to its small neighboring village. We are the first Americans back in this jungle region since the war's end.

> Thin smoke rising
> from the wooden hut—
> only cooking

We are guided to his old outpost. The triple canopy jungle is gone. The concertina wire, tanks, foxholes all gone. We survey crop fields that fade in the forest's edge. The Vietnamese "beat swords into ploughshares." Everything we left behind is used.

> Chopper skid marks
> buried beneath
> drying tubers

He remembers the high, deep, solemn mood of the jungle.

> Greatest fear —
> jungle sunset —
> greatest beauty

We meet a former Viet Cong soldier resting in a crowd of workers.

> Stooping in the mud
> telling old stories
> on a metal leg

We call at a small cemetery for VC war dead beside the old runways.

> Lighting incense
> for those he feared
> over their graves

Remembrance pebbles for his own dead comrades in his palms, he surveys the low jungle one last time.

> Where last he saw
> a village burning
> tears burn his eyes

Back in the hotel, alone in his room,

> His enemy's eyes
> staring into him
> in the mirror

—∞∞∞—

I travel into Viet Nam's central region, where time-carved mountains twist in jagged contortions into a sun-washed sky. In the cool shadows of deep grottos, life and death struggles were fought with weapons and prayers.

Marble Mountain, outside Da Nang, was given this simple name by GIs. It is a five mountain group that erupts from the coastal plain, known to the peasantry as The Mountain and the Sea and to scholars as The Mountain of the Five Essential Elements. We climb the Mountain of Water.

Marble Mountain

I climb the steep, carved stairway snaking through the marble causeways. I arrive at the first of several Buddhist pagodas. A veteran's daughter, who says she has never before entered a non-Christian place of worship, steps forward to be enveloped by chanting monks.

> White feet on clay tile—
> crossing Buddha's threshold
> crossing herself

In another pagoda, I meet a young man who was conscripted for the invasion of Cambodia. Afterwards, he wandered barefoot across Viet Nam, his singular goal after wartime service to find a monastery that would accept him as a novice.

> In saffron robes
> the monk remembers
> shooting at the sky

Inside the great cavern a huge statue of Buddha looks down on the stone chapel once used by guerillas as a field hospital until it was brutally attacked:

> Below Buddha's gaze
> the ten thousand things
> inscribed with bullets

Standing in contemplation, I am surrounded by a flood of school children.

> Praying for war to end—
> laughing children skip
> down carved marble stairs

I descend to the mountain's feet and walk through the village coated end to end in the white marble dust of its souvenir industry.

> The street child begs
> for a gift—
> my sweaty bandana

Again I travel to the irrigation ditch and the scattering of house mounds that would be unknown but for what we did here.

My Lai

> Bright-eyed boy
> playing peek-a-boo
> on his grandmother's grave

I meet an elderly gardener, snipping weeds, whose entire family died on that day.

> Beyond the ditch
> where my daughters died—
> new green rice

She says she wishes she had died with them.

> Each snip
> of her rusty scissors
> a gun blast

What can we do to ease her pain? How does she feel about our visit?

> You wish to help me heal?
> Please let me
> forgive you

———— ∞ ————

As I travel from mountain to sea, from city to village, jungle to paddy, and old firebase site to thronging market, faces, encounters, stories collect like an album of snapshots. The very word itself is telling; a snapshot was originally a quick, unaimed shot with a gun.

Snapshots

My friend and guide Tran Dinh Song tells me of the first time his mother, on a market trip from her mountain village, encountered a cold treat she was sure her son would love.

> She wraps sweet ice cream
> in fresh banana leaves
> and hikes to her far village
> with this gift for her son

On every street of every town, vendors who have no other work greet or chase every potential customer.

> "Buy something, friend."
> He presses my hand
> between warm stumps

I again visit my friend in Hoi An, Do Thanh Son, a young sculptor who would rather go hungry reading philosophy than carve the stone souvenirs that allow his family to eat. I tour his tiny shop.

> Sharpened steel strut
> of a rotting U.S. tank—
> his chiseling tool

A woman veteran and I cross mountain peaks where we survey great vistas of forest and seacoast.

> In thick white clouds
> small pines speckle burned soil—
> the old nurse's tears

In a remote village, I am invited into an old man's tiny wood frame home to meet his granddaughter and stand before his family altars memorializing his parents, wife, and two sons killed fighting Americans.

> Incense, candles, fruit—
> his two sons in black and white
> fading

I arrive again in Ha Noi, long time capital first shown to Ly Thai To, a Vietnamese king, 1,000 years ago by a dragon that burst from its lake waters and flew to the sky. *Ta Vong*, the lake in the center of the proud city, once hosted the golden tortoise, messenger of the Emperor of Waters. Now the mists of night, the buzz of noisy crowds, the lights of modernity mingle with legend and history.

Ha Noi

> On the still lake's midnight surface
> a glowing tower competes with the full moon.
> On its unseen bottom a giant tortoise breathes.
> Reflections shimmer so brightly
> I do not know which to watch.
> In the nearby pagoda
> amid wafting incense smoke
> a gong awaits its mallet.

IV: ICE MOON SETTING

2002

My co-leader Steven Leibo has been wandering Asia since the war days. For decades he has been greeting the dawn on Asian bridges. He first introduced our early morning ritual on the bridge over the Sai Gon River.

We begin this journey as we did the others, in Ho Chi Minh City again, rising with the sun to stand among the throngs on foot, bicycle, cyclo, or moped crossing the Khanh Hoi Bridge.

Rush Hour

Like light straining to pierce an oldster's cataracts
the white fireball of morning greets me
through a hazy sky. It is my third year
of days begun on this simple span of concrete
arching across the gray-green river.
The small of my sagging back
is supported by the same span that upholds
these thousands. I stand here, white and alone,
in a sea of flowing tan droplets,
in a torrent of falling yellow rain,
on a face flooding with ochre tears.
They are stares. They are nods. They are grins.
Their eyes are questions, dances, blessings.
It is for me to come, year after year,
to stand and greet through their rush hour.
It is for me to carry new things, things that smile
to this place where we cargo-ed endless tears.
It is for me, on this teeming morning bridge,
to join the sun in burning off
the nightmares, the cataracts, the old fears
that keep me alone, that prevent us from becoming
a single sea, a single sky, a single face.

— ∞ —

I visit Reunification Hall. It was the old presidential palace until April 30, 1975, when its gates were forced open by Russian-built T-54 tanks leading the victorious Northern forces. Next to me a former American ranger stands in front of the lead tank and remembers:

Tanks

"They don't exist,"
his officers insisted
until the fire-belching steel
crushed their wire,
their guns,
his friends.
He stands before them
goosebumped again,
taking pictures.

———⚬⚬⚬———

With the privatizing on the marketplace and growth of tourism, Thai and Japanese foot massage parlors are becoming popular with both foreigners and some successful Vietnamese businessmen who can afford them. Young men and women from the north or the countryside clamber for these long hour, low paying jobs that give them, through tips and the people they might meet, the small seeds of hope for a better life in the city.

Massage Girl

First of five daughters—
my parents plant young rice sprouts
I knead your muscles

Fourteen hours a day
my father plants, sows, harvests
I soothe weary feet

My father's rice paddies
thick with green sprouts
and rusting shrapnel

Among sputtering mopeds
how I miss
our plodding buffalo

One day each month—
my only holiday—
the long ride home

$20 monthly wage
for my room, clothes, food—
tips to carry home

My mother
land, sisters, ancestors —
tears on my pillow

My father and you—
half a century same same—
how are you so young?

My brown skin—
the flag of the weary poor—
will you make a trade?

My story—
your smile —
happiness

———∞∞∞———

In a country swelling with new vibrancy and pride, it is easy to forget those who suffered from the southern defeat. Through the crowded streets and before a museum's war photographs, my 40 year old cyclo driver dubs me "elder brother" and in clumsy, vivid English reminds me.

Cyclo Driver

Colonel my father
long sword hanging from his belt—
men and I salute

Zip zip through the sky
leading steel birds of flame—
I play in the dirt

VC bang bang
tearing apart his plane
and my heart

My mother wailing—
I must walk tall
carrying his bones

Hat, shoulder bars, sword —
my mother's memory chest
in our far village

Peddling all day—
I don't march, I don't plow—
thighs ache and ache

I listen—
revolutionary songs—
I don't sing

From its ashes
my phoenix
does not rise

———— ∞ ————

In a typical afternoon downpour that squeezes humidity out of the torpid
air, I walk with both veterans and civilians through crowded streets to a
poor section of Ho Chi Minh City. Tiny storefronts crammed with goods
by day become one-room houses by night. Goods are stacked against the
walls as extended family members jam together on their sleeping mats.

Amidst stalls of tools, foodstuffs, clothing, we find the scattering of
vendors selling war surplus items or their cheap imitations left over from
French, American, Chinese, Northern and Southern armies. Infamous
Zippo lighters are everywhere—"real $20, fake $2."

War Relics Market

Prowling the stalls—
helmets, ditty bags, uniforms—
no weapons

Northern pilot's cap
flaps dangling over my ears—
old men's laughter

Old beret
awaiting
my winter

Stacks of black and white
torn from wallets and albums—
my trembling fingers

Above the VC scarf
soft smile, black eyes—
killer hero girl friend

A dozen dog tags—
real or fake?
ghost of a squad

This stranger's name
riding home in my wallet
this brother's name

—⚬⚬⚬—

Eight Americans, men and women, vets and civilians, pick our ways through heat and traffic. We arrive at the busy intersection where in 1963 Buddhist monk Thich Quang Duc immolated himself to protest the Southern regime's religious oppression and war frenzy. I bow before the humble memorial altar built on a street corner and protected from the stampede by a flimsy fence. I contemplate his act and our compulsion to honor it.

Prayer

When

I

burn

let

me

sit

—⚬⚬⚬—

It is my last sunset in Viet Nam's largest city. The laughing boatman's firm grasp helps me leap from the dock and climb the roof of his caique. As the disappearing sun drags its light from the sky, the river night opens hidden windows on Ho Chi Minh City.

Night on the Sai Gon River

Quickly the thick green water
becomes as dark as the sky —
only the lines of glowing neon
and floating garbage separate them.
Our unpainted wooden boat, worn smooth,
two large eyes above the water line,
sputters, plows and plods, piercing the darkness
and picking its way between tankers,
trawlers, water taxis, and the teeming,
crumbling houseboats built of wooden poles,
corrugated, rusted steel, cardboard sheets,
endless rows of flapping rags.

Why am I so happy
on this river of crowded darkness
picking my way between the smells
of bobbing, rotting garbage
and frying fish and greens?
Why am I so happy
peeling the thick red chum-chums,
rolling their juicy full moon fruit
on my acrid tongue? Why am I content,
sandwiched between the flashing signs of global business
and the ancient, endless toil of the poor?
Carried on this current that has carried
millions from arms of flesh to beds of earth,
from distant cool mountains, through flooded paddies,
to the common, undifferentiated sea,
am I the servant
or am I the one being served?

Tay Ninh Snapshots

I travel again through Tay Ninh province, once the severely battered Iron Triangle. I am welcomed into the home of Phan Thanh Tam. On this narrow road, outside this very house where I now sip his coffee, he was the boy running beside his sister Kim Phuc in the photo of scorched children. Now he proudly introduces his own daughters who are the age he and Kim were when they became famous.

> Left eye
> seared blind by napalm
> above his toothless grin

I arrive in Lady Black's mountaintop pagoda. In the distance, the blue-gray mountains of Cambodia wiggle in the heat. I stand before the icons of Lady Black and the omnipresent Quan Am, Vietnamese incarnation of the Goddess of Mercy.

> Still air, beating sun
> kneeling before their goddess
> a gust grabs my cap

A long mountain slide has recently been opened that twists and meanders above the crevices of shrine and battlefield. As I climb aboard for the breezy descent, I wonder —does this goddess hear our prayers?

> Between these boulders
> fire scars, bullet casings,
> children's laughter

I return to the Mekong Delta, so fertile that its farmers squeeze three rice harvests a year from its paddies while the north manages only two. My boat sputters along its snaking waterways, past laboring fishermen, swimming children, sampans loaded with jungle fruit.

Delta Daughter

She stoops on her bobbing raft
behind her father's dragging pole,
her smile, her wave, her bright pink blouse
the single blossom dawning
in this world of dripping green.

—⁂—

The depth of greenery and fertility make our war seem long ago and far away. But the tall jungle is gone; this green is new growth. Peel it back and both land and people reveal secrets and scars. A Vietnamese veteran confides:

Duty

Behind the dirt dyke
the crumbling VC bunker—
my grandfather's grave.
On holy days I feast both
ancestors and wanderers.

—⁂—

Again I sleep, again awaken in a cot between veterans and civilians in a guesthouse over the river. Again the darkness that once held terror seems infinite and hidden life is revealed through what we cannot see.

The Veteran Awakens

Scurrying and stuttering geckos,
mosquito netting fluttering before the fan,
canvas cot hugging his sagging butt,
diamonds of sky fire peeking through wall slats—
he smiles a Buddha smile. It's all the same
as his last sleep here three decades ago.
All the same save for the sunrise chatter
of those who do not know this darkness,
who did not sleep in it before
electricity, music, friendship,
who never learned its lurking death.
He smiles to know what they cannot:
never blather in the dawn;
never fail to daily mouth
the blessing of awakening
as you breathe this thick and humid air
for one more morning, one more prayer.

—⚬⚬⚬—

I have traveled half the world and half a century to swim this ancient murky river without fear and to sit on this rail porch as dawn slowly draws its curtain open to reveal mystery in simplicity. Amidst rooster caws and changing colors, I watch the first ice delivery I have seen since my family moved from our tenement apartment half a century ago.

Ice Moon

Yellow moon face rises
before the white blaze of sun
tops the low green palms.
She floats downriver against the far sea tide
to load her narrow sampan with frozen blocks
of river cleansed of its fertile silt.
Then she turns with the salt tide
to sputter upstream, house-hopping
with her straining arms. Her sickle moon saw
carves the cold into chunks that will drip
and drip through the long humid day,
cooling what we drink against the steam and sweat.
She leaves three clear bricks on our worn plank ramp.
They stand sentinel to the climbing blaze
now burning the palms to green torches.
Then she turns to sputter away again,
ice moon setting in thick green clumps
of hyacinth pushed by the tide upriver
toward the mountains she will never see.

———∞———

To the Vietnamese, the South China Sea is not named after the northern giant that so often invaded and occupied their lands. Vietnamese call it the Eastern Sea, home and element of their ancestral father the Dragon, who brings the waters that make their land fertile. I travel to Vung Tau, on the coast southeast of Ho Chi Minh City. Once French colonial rulers retreated there for beauty and called it Cap St. Jacques. Later wounded Americans were sent there to recuperate. One vet, who was temporarily blinded in an ambush, was sent there to heal and await transport home. As we travel together, he sees Vung Tau for the first time. Beside an impoverished village, pristine beaches grow into a resort.

Vung Tau

Raindrops pound the steely waves.
Waves roll out of the blind horizon.
Water falls. Waves roil as thick
as rice flying in their winnowing fans.
Jet skis and beach umbrellas dissolve.
Only the slow steady water buffalo
plod these smooth streets, their hooves
puncturing the prickling rain.

—⚭—

After the storm, I climb rain-slick stone steps up many levels of pagoda,
each with its Buddha or Quan Am altar, ascending a bell tower standing
as if on watch for the return of the dragon from the sea. This solemn
seaside temple is dubbed *Niet Ban*, which means Nirvana in Vietnamese.

In the Niet Ban Temple

On the cracked steps
the incense peddler
black teeth above bristled chin
kisses my hand for the purchase.

Before the bronze bell
the kowtowing nun
scalp cloaked with gray bristles
mutters prayers for my prayer.

I stand beneath
the two soft hands
and the downturned vessel
of this goddess pouring mercy.

—⚭—

She was Viet Cong. She painted a past moment of such tranquility or exhaustion that the terror is hardly noticed:

VC Memory

Swinging in her hammock
between banana trees
cradling her AK

———— ✸ ————

I travel with Bill, whose army ranger unit patrolled My Lai three days before the massacre. Villagers gave him food and water. His squad found nothing suspicious. As we walk through My Lai together, he tells of his shock and rage upon hearing of the massacre after he had reported a friendly village. Then, when she is sure we want to know, the young woman who is our guide responds with her story.

My Lai Guide

Kettle, flame, scattered straw.
Dawn breaks. My great aunt cooks rice.
Her three children play and hug her legs.

Kettle dumped, flames galloping through straw.
Dawn burns. My aunt's face twists.
Three days before she had given them rice.

Their last moment before your people
landed in the paddies behind her hut —
their last hour as your people
taunted them beside the ditch.
These two moments are photographs
I can neither blend nor dissolve.

I left for college.
I left to learn your language.
I left to burn these photos.
But I want to die here too.
Until I do I will tell the story.
Their last moment must last forever.

I stay in Hoi An, a coastal town between My Lai and Da Nang. During the colonial era it was an important port. Now it is renowned for its silk and tailoring. Middle aged boatwomen, who look much older than their years, ask 10,000 *dong*, about 70c, for an hour's boat ride and tell of running as children from our bombing, strafing and defoliating planes.

Hospitality

When Heaven spills on our paddies
or swells our river, we rejoice.
But the only water
in what you dropped on my childhood
dripped from my cheeks as I fled.

Now you sit on the rotting plank seat
of my puttering boat
as we cruise between these river banks together.
This time no one flees
and it is not my cheeks that drip.

My feet fly me to the closet-sized shop of my friend Son, the young sculptor whose name means Mountain. A scholar in love with philosophy, language and literature, he had to drop out of college in order to support his ailing elderly parents and his mad older brother. The Vietnamese use our arcane term "mad" for those numberless offspring who, at any age from infancy through adolescence, due to the long-term effects of Agent Orange, deteriorate in physical or mental functioning into complete incapacity.

I find Son's tiny shop on a busy main thoroughfare between clothing stores and cold drink vendors.

Closed

The old black padlock on his worn plank door
would not halt a determined gecko.
Behind this sun-splashed pale wood
are stacks of worn, finger-stained books—
Poe, Hemingway, James, Shakespeare—
written in words he can understand but not pronounce.
His stacks are piled between the three squat walls
he built with his old father,
lined with thinly shaved shelves,
like an ancient temple
displaying rows of Buddhas, saints, goddesses
smiling, smiling, smiling.
He toils to chip and shape their grins
from his marble chunks—
pink from the south,
red from Ha Noi,
and yellow from the mountains near his central home.
He caresses these chunks of his homeland
the way a gentle breeze ripples the rice grass.

I cannot find my friend today.
From the side of the world
he imagines but can never see
I carried his favorite gift—
books and hours of talk
in a language he loves but cannot speak.
Now I am the gecko by his door
squatting in the steaming noon
in dust, scattered leaves, moped drone,
waiting for an hour as he waits for a year.

I listen to the crickets click
as sweat drips from my nose and brow.
A lone bird lands in the dusty tree
and warbles the song we would speak:
"It is the sap root. It is the sap root."
Though I have the language he craves
I cannot pronounce the name of this ache
I carry for this hour a year of talk with my friend.
The crickets halt. The bird flies away.
The ache will travel everywhere I go.
What does gifting him gift me?

In the simmering summer noon, the sidewalks become radiators and both
vendors and customers desert the marketplace.

Hoi An Noon

"Hello! Sir! Boat ride!"
Her only English echoes through the steam
as she steers and bumps her tiny sampan
beneath the carved hull and long rudder
of the two-decker tourist boat.
"Hello. Sir. Boat ride."
Her right hand grips her push pole
or tugs the tour boat's anchor line.
Her left hand lifts and drops, lifts and drops
as between calls she drags on a cigarette.
"Hello. Sir. Boat ride."
Streets empty. Stalls closed. Too hot even for vendors.
She cannot risk missing a single fare.
But I have had my daily ferry.
Shade is all she has.
"Hello. Sir. Boat ride."

I finally locate my friend Son. Once again he sits me in his seat of honor —the only rickety chair in his tiny shop. Before we talk "of cabbages and kings" he explains why he is now often out of his shop and difficult to locate.

Reunion

It has been a hard year.
First my old grandfather, survivor
of floods, famines and four wars, died.
Then my uncle, suddenly.
Finally my father fell ill.
For weeks I sat by his side in hospital
but by Tet he was gone.
His funeral took all the money we had.
I could not think. I could not work.
I could not feed my mother and brother.
And that is why, after September 11,
though I worried about you I did not write.
I have examined my mistake.
Now I ask you, please, friend,
can you forgive me?

We can never know when the gates of memory will part another inch. But the return of forgotten scenes of tenderness or humor are green shoots on dry twigs—signs of healing. Perhaps awakened by the hospitality we find throughout Viet Nam, one of my traveling companions who, during the war, helped supply the young men who would fight to survive, recalls:

Quartermaster's Memory

Once a month without fail
beneath the green canopy
beneath layers of sticky tape
inside boxes inside boxes
I had to bayonet open—
fresh Wonder Bread and a note,
"Love, Dad."

My Hoi An days recede as we climb the coast-hugging mountain road snaking north. Monkey Mountain rises out of the Eastern Sea, a green explosion from an aqua bed. My bus stops at a summit called The Pass Above the Clouds. We seem poised on a precipice between north and south, past and present, grief and hope.

The Pass Above the Clouds

Old gun emplacements and watchtowers, built by the French and used in both their war and ours, line the horizon. I peer through machine gun slits that shrink the verdant vista to a peephole.

Concrete bunker
riddled with bullet holes —
the smell of buffalo dung

One companion is a student of military history. Like so many old warriors, he joins his story to those who struggled before him and draws one inevitable conclusion:

American veteran
pointing out the positions
of the dead French

Another vet, in a lighter mood, has bought from a vendor and joins us on the ridge.

> Beneath the power line
> and the abandoned grave
> munching his Pringles

Today younger as well as adult vendors meet our bus. My wife Kate befriends a young woman who dreams of college.

> School holiday —
> trudging up the long hill
> to sell trinkets

Vets, civilians, Vietnamese stand together on the ridge overlooking valley and sea, as if we can survey the scope of history and destiny we finally share.

> Scanning the mountains
> where rustling leaves meant danger
> purple wildflowers

—— ✺ ——

My companions depart to buy or take cover from vendors and sun in our bus. But I push on to explore the high ridge. I wander among now-silent bunkers and forever-bursting flowers.

In A Mountain Pass

On this stone ledge above an emerald valley
I stoop before a lone grave
with its carpet of red incense stumps
and crumbling yellow cement block
where a name tablet should be.
Whom do I remember
in this shroud of blue butterflies,
whom do I grieve?

———ೲ———

In Hue, we boat upriver to visit Thien Mu Pagoda, perched on the banks of the Perfume River. I pass through its entryway, tapping the largest bronze bell in Viet Nam, hugging a giant marble statue of a tortoise. Long a teaching center of the union of spirituality and social activism, Thien Mu is the home pagoda of Thich Quang Duc, who burned himself in protest in 1963, and of world-renowned peace activist Thich Nhat Hanh. The old sedan that Quang Duc drove from this sanctuary to the Sai Gon intersection of his immolation stands in these grounds as a memorial.

Thien Mu in Vietnamese means Celestial Lady. On this site, an Empress of Heaven promised Nguyen Huang, a medieval king, that his devotion and sacrifice would guarantee a legacy of independence to his children.

Thien Mu Pagoda

A purple lotus blooms —a cloud-borne lady
descends to this rock and greets her king,
"Your children can be freed with your blood."

A purple lotus blooms —a simple monk
abandons this rock to send his ruler
a prayer scroll of flesh freed from fear by fire.

A purple lotus blooms —his old sedan
is an altar for clicking cameras.
All colors bow in the wafting incense.

A purple lotus blooms —I step between
the gong and the bow, the mantra and the flame.
Perfect petals teach me my imperfection.

Viet Nam reputedly esteems women more than any other Asian culture.
In Ha Noi the Army Museum honors the thousands of women who lost
three or more male relations during the war. A Woman's Museum docu-
ments, and art galleries and other museums portray, their overwhelming
degrees and kinds of devotion and sacrifice. And everywhere, from crowded
cities to remote hamlets, I meet women missing arms and legs, women
whose tiny homes are dominated by altars of their deceased relatives,
women who look a score of years older than their age, women whose
faces are a jungle of Agent Orange tumors. Yet everywhere they welcome
us and speak of forgiveness.

Song of the Vietnamese Women

I will grow my rice beside your craters.
I will place my body before your tanks.
I will give my hands to stop your helicopters
and give my legs to cut your wire.
I will mark your minefields to protect my village.
and hoe all day to stand watch all night.
I will dig and chop and lash and haul
to open jungle trails to foil you.

I will go without rice so our fighters may eat
and sing in the foxholes beneath your burning rain.
I will wrap myself in chains to show what you do
and bandage your wounds when you fall into my arms.
I will give my father, my husband, my sons
and bless their leaving though I never see them again.
I will pray you return to your mothers' arms
and forgive you though you take everything I have.

I will feed my men whose hands you have shorn.
I will carry my sisters through the bleeding night.
I will tend my buffalo as your bombs fall down
and rebuild my dykes after you have blown them.
I will aim my plow as straight as my gun
and plant young rice and forge new bullets.
Long after you are gone and have forgotten me
I will give my limbs to defuse your mines.

Made for feeding, caressing, sowing,
made for nursing, carrying, caring,
made for planting, harvesting, cooking,
made for threading, weaving, sewing,
made for singing, dancing, laughing,
made for acting, playing, loving,
come here with hatred and I will don
the helmet, the scope, the rifle, the bomb.

I am grandmother, mother, wife, daughter.
Make me angry and you cannot be right.
Make me mad and you cannot be just.
Make me rebel though all I am
wishes to birth and plant and grow,
make me resist and you show your heart.
Make me fight and you cannot win.
Make me stand and you will fall.
Return in peace and show me your wounds
and I will bind them with love and call you brother.

———

In a guest house on the Mekong River, on a barge on the Perfume River, on a full moon night along the riverbank in Hoi An, in a concert hall beside Ha Noi's Lake of the Sword Restoration —in all these places I listen to musicians weaving the enduring sounds and strains of *Ca Dao*, traditional Vietnamese poem-folksongs, as it praises and laments rice and rain and love:

> As many as the strands of a bridge
> So are the sorrows of my heart.

And warns or grieves of war and drought and danger:

> When the tom tom gives the alarm
> with one foot in the boat
> our tears fall like rain.

Its plucking strings and plaintiff cries play and play until a voice and song play within me.

Lullaby

Because you are far away, my son,
and I am an old woman alone
I listen in my quiet hours
to raindrops flicking lotus petals.
In this way, though you are gone, the patter
of your tiny feet fills my empty home.

V: THE LEGEND OF KING LE LOI

Introduction

Myths and legends simultaneously record history, reveal psychology, preserve and promote culture, and illuminate a people's spirit and soul. Thus, we only truly arrive in another culture when we penetrate its mythology. When we grasp a myth, discover what is universal about it, and find ourselves in it, we truly become friends as what was foreign becomes another home.

King Le Loi was one of the great figures of Vietnamese history and legend. His tale has remarkable similarities to heroic tales and foundational myths from all over the world. In the English speaking world, it has special similarities to tales of both King Arthur and George Washington. Like Arthur's, it is complete with a magical sword akin to Excaliber and a golden tortoise akin to the Lady of the Lake who reclaims the sword. Like both Arthur's and Washington's, it is the story of a man of the land who led a heroic rebellion, became the freed people's ruler, and united fractionalized regions into one country and vision. All these legends transmit the themes of divine guidance and purpose, eternal friendship, personal and national identities defamed, discovered and restored, and the struggle to build a legitimate, independent and just country during both war and peace.

The culture hero's daunting and harmonizing adventure, the essence of the epic form, is universal. Herein, Le Loi tells us his Vietnamese tale in English language epic verse. This effort helps reconcile and unite what history sundered.

Notes accompany the poem to guide readers in understanding Vietnamese myths, history and customs detailed in the poem, and in comparing this myth with others of similar theme and content. Some details vary in different versions of Le Loi's myth. Such variations, mentioned in the notes, inevitably occur in myths descending from oral traditions. I first heard many parts of this tale verbally retold by friends, guides, teachers and acquaintances in various regions of Viet Nam. As long as they are true to tradition and the overall coherence and integrity of the story, the varying details are less important than the cumulative vision and message. All versions retain the essential story. Readers who wish to give their swords to the golden tortoise and build peace, reconciliation, and friendship between Viet Nam and America will find that it is their story too.

The Legend of King Le Loi

I

I lived in a hut near the turbulent sea.
Daily as I fished the dragon's tail whipped foam in my face.
Nightly as I tossed the dragon's breath rustled my thatched roof.
It seemed to be restless. It seemed to be calling.
It seemed to be crying. It had not laid its eggs
in a hatchery for slaves. It had not given birth
to one hundred children, nor spoken to kings,
so that we would carry the names of slaves.[1]
I thought I could hear this but I was afraid.
I was just a poor fisherman. What could I do?[2]

Not now, but more years than the scales on a dragon—
not now, but more years than we tend our ancestors —
that long the invaders had eaten our rice,
stolen our sons, forced us to use their words
and their alphabet, called our home Pacified,
a slave name with no honor.[3] In mountains and villages
my brothers rebelled, sharpening bamboo,
chipping stones, shaping bows. In small bands and large
they bid farewell to their wives and children
and charged and fought or dodged and hid.[4]

But I seemed made of bones, my wife and children
all bones. It was all I could do, year upon year,
to haul my sampan to the sea, to row
against tides, to drag my nets through surf
and dump their load on the deck of my boat.
I looked with longing at my rebel brothers.
My heart shed tears for their vacant huts.
My blood boiled oil when the invaders
torched a neighbor's home or snatched my catch
to feed their hoards that chained our land.

When the Emperor cries out we must not refuse.
My heart beat like grandfather's bronze drum
when he called the dragon to bring the rains.[5]
I tossed in the nights. I towed through the tides.
I hauled in my nets though shriveling from toil.
One night the dragon's roar boiled the moon.
I did not sleep yet weary I rowed,
weary I tossed, weary I hauled the net
that seemed to grow heavier as if the sea
would drag me in and make me its food.

So be it! I thought. Let the dragon eat me.
Free me from slavery. Make me your egg.
So be it! My heart gave up. One final yank
would swallow me. I pulled my last pull
against tide and foam, glad to drown quickly
and not be a slave. But instead of swallowing
the dragon spit. Like a flying moon
my tangled net leapt from the sea.
I kowtowed as it clanged on my deck.
This is how gods speak. Then who am I?

II[6]

I untangled the strange iron blade from my net.
For weeks I stared as it lay on my altar
where I placed it before my father,
grandfather, and his father too.[7]
I lit extra incense, the odd number three
that we give to the spirits when all is in question.[8]
I asked them to speak and answer this riddle —
tell me the meaning of this blade from the sea.
The dragon continued to roar day and night,
crying its pain. But it did not answer.

Far worse than not knowing what to do
is not doing what one knows one must.
Far worse than not knowing who one is
is feeling a destiny that will not unfold.
Our sea is the dragon, our ancestor, our sperm.
Our sea calm and stormy is worshipped forever
as father of our people. The sea had spit forth
a tool not of my trade but a warrior's.
But if Father could only rage against slavery,
then Mother, dear Mother, might guide her lost son.

I turned to the mountains where the fairy lives.
I turned to the mountains whose clouds are their crowns,
whose gray mist is breath, whose jungles are cloaks
of green swathing for our fairy mother's arms.
She too had been silent, breathing in pain.
Her tea plants were broken, their leaves unreadable.
Into her jungle of thick hanging vines,
of mud paths and swamps, of snakes and of bats,
I plunged, I pushed, I plodded without rice.
Answer me, Mother! Who is your son?

In deep jungle darkness where I breathed green air,
where steep slopes are made of slick green rocks,
where before me only fairies dared tread,
there in the green air where earth breathed its sorrow,
no food in my belly, no hope in my chest,
in the midst of a grove of emerald-leafed bamboo,
poles longer, more sections, than bamboo can grow,
a light, a golden light, not of this world,
shone like the sun buried in earth,
shone like the breath of the Mother herself.[9]

Again I bowed deeply, this time to Mother.
The light seemed to shine through my palms and it burned.
I clutched. I coiled. I became like the snake,
churning the soil to escape from all threat.
Loam flew from my fingers, and grubs and roots,
until deep in earth's body my fingers hit metal,
firm and cool, long and true, shaped to a purpose.
Mother threw me the sheath of a warrior
inscribed with two names, my best friend's and mine,
followed by titles I dared not utter.[10]

III

Home again. Home again. Legs flying home.
Down rock slopes. Through mangroves. Past woodcutter's huts.
I clutched the dank bundle, my gift from the earth.
I did not know or guess the Emperor's purpose
but as I ran and stumbled and ran once more
I saw in clear light that The Land and the Water —
the name of our country, elements of our parents —
cried as they rattled the chains of our slavery.[11]
At home without food, without thought, without fear
I fell before the altar of all we hold dear.

Incense wafting, ancestors fed, wife worried for my life
reassured and asleep, I took out the casing
from beneath my rags. I stroked it and hugged it
and read it once more. My name and my friend's
in letters of gold —like the light, like the breath,
like the heart of the dragon. My fingers
trembled as I lifted it high. My heart
halted between past and future, despair and elation,
enslavement and action. One final prayer
and I lifted the sword. Of its own it leapt home.

A sword in its scabbard is a heart in its home,
a people in their land, a dream in its act.
Still I dared not speak. For days my family
had had no fish, for weeks I had seemed strange.
Now I began to believe the impossible
and went in search of the friend of my youth.[12]
Far wiser than I, with eyes made of onyx,
a mind like a mountain river in spring,
he listened in silence, he nodded, he prayed.
When the Emperor speaks we dare not refuse.

My friend said to wait and sent me home.
He told me to fish in the sea and the river.
He told me to watch —when dragon was ready
we should be ready. Until then the sword
must hide its prediction in a poor man's rags.
He went to the mountains with buckets of honey
and the tiny brushes made for a scholar.
While I fished, while I watched, while the dragon still screamed,
he lettered the sweet words found on the scabbard
in dripping bee's gold on hundreds of leaves.

Ants are the soldiers and workers who teach
how to build villages and cities as one.
Ants found the honey. Ants ate the letters.
Ants who build cities now wrote the words
announced by the mountain, spoken by sea,
into the leaves of the forest in fall.
Wise friend! Winds blew. Cold climbed the hills.
Leaves fell, floated, tumbled, shod the feet
of our people. Now everyone knew. Miracle
of shrewdness, his first public deed.

IV

The people rose up, chains of fear snapped,
and marched to my village an army of ants.
They cried my name, insisted I lead.
Only then did I take the sword from my rags,
only then strap it on, only then tell the tale.
The dragon will lead us, the mountain give strength,
the sword of the two made one by their children.
Freedom was born then, long before battle.
Freedom was born in the dream of a people
chained too long by kings with no love.

Battle is horror. I never will praise it.
I always felt pity for each fish I took.
Invaders were many with their wagons and swords.
We remembered their cruelty of twelve hundred years.
The sword led the way with its power and its light.
It was not I and I never will claim it.
The words of the mountain, the blade of the sea,
the dream of a people, the faith of a friend,
these became one as one became dragon
and carved through all trouble. Our enemies fled.

I established my kingdom, friend by my side,
like a smashed porcelain teapot with love restored,
all people welcome from city and shore,
all dragon's children from the same bag.
We sowed and we built, we sang and made laws.
I stayed near the sea to remember the tides.
I traveled to mountains, jungles and plains,
villages, hamlets, collecting all strays,
making us one as ants are one colony,
all dragon's children from the same bag.[13]

I ever loved fishing. I always loved fish
and studied the currents and tested the waters.
Wearing the sword of the Emperor of Water
I never forgot who I was by myself.
One night on a boat above the Red River,
stars blazing like scales on a great dragon's flanks,
my friend beside me, my guards all around,
I lowered my king's body to the hard wooden planks.
As close as I could stoop to my origins
I kowtowed forehead to deck to give thanks.

My people say that when we see a dragon
in dreamtime it means the Emperor gives nod.
Some call it a dream, for others no name
but a vision of something more real than life.
Bowed to the ground of the lake in my boat
I saw what our King saw rise from the deep.
Scales of gold, wings of flame, eyes of sparkling jade,
the dragon leapt from water to sky.
His tail and his wake wrote across Heaven
that our people and freedom would never die.

V

Here, said my friend, I must build my center.
So there I planted temples, schools and laws
till they grew and they glowed like new young rice.
When invaders stampede on our rice and our dreams
future rulers will wield the soul of my sword.
The dragon will guide them forever to rise.
Rising Dragon showed it. Our king named it for him.[14]
The rice was now ours. Our home was now free.
Contented I boarded my old wooden boat.
Contented I floated beneath a full moon.

The lake was a looking glass kissed by the goddess.
The sky showed the sparkle of the great dragon's teeth.
My friend by my side, our rowers all nodding,
I thought all was done. I thought rest was mine.
But I have learned this from the hardships of fishing,
of war and of ruling —never think yourself done.
Relax in a calm sea —a storm will soon follow.
Think yourself safe and your throne may be lost.
Beneath the calm surface that mirrored my kingship
as of old I heard the dragon roil and cry.

A great pointed head broke the lake's surface.
Like the scales of a dragon a huge shell appeared.
Did I sin? Lose faith? I thought it a monster
and grabbed the strong hilt of my sword from the sea.
I raised it high as I had against Ming.
It flashed in the moon and my name flashed with light.
I was ready to strike to protect the dragon
so long forced to wear the chains of a slave.
Tip to the sky, I gathered my power
of casting and seeking, of striking and building.

"Oh king," cried a voice of thunder and jasmine.
"Great Emperor," cried my heart in terror and awe.
"Do not strike," said the sky through the mouth of the turtle.
The tortoise stared into me with eyes like the sword —
piercing, invincible, cutting to bone.
I remembered the sea that first threw the blade.
I remembered the mountain that first cried my name.
Sea dragon our father, mountain fairy our mother —
Tortoise is created of mountain and sea.

I watched turtle's green shell become golden,
golden his beak, claws, tail and sharp eyes.
Under the moon all my city was pale
while tortoise radiated the ancient gold light.
And I saw at once that all we are
are pale shadows of truth, shades of a will
that runs through all time and composes the tales
that we must enact to assist the one king.
In turtle's mouth I placed my great sword.
More than God gives us, we must return.

Notes to The Legend of King Le Loi

[1] The dragon is the ruling spirit and ancestral father of the Vietnamese people. He is *Long Quan*, Dragon King, Emperor of the Water, whose realm is the sea. The myth of the origins of the Vietnamese people is that Long Quan married *Au Co*, the mountain fairy, who gave birth to 100 eggs in one sack. These hatched into their children. 50 children returned to the mountains with Au Co, becoming the indigenous mountain tribes of Viet Nam. 50 returned to the sea with Long Quan, becoming the Viet people. Viet Nam literally means the Country of the Southern Viets.

[2] Some folk versions of this myth say that Le Loi was originally a poor fisherman. Historically it is believed that he was a landowner from Thanh Hoa province south of Ha Noi. The fisherman is also said to have been *Le Than* who later gave Le Loi, as leader of the rebellion, the sword blade.

[3] The Chinese name for Viet Nam was Annam, which means The Pacified South. The Chinese occupied Viet Nam for almost 1,200 years, from 179 BCE to 938 CE. For centuries following the initial liberation, the Chinese invaded again and again, sometimes occupying parts of Viet Nam for periods of time and over time absorbing the northern Viet people.

Historically Le Loi's rebellion was against an especially cruel 20 year occupation by the Ming dynasty, 1407-1427. Le Loi claimed kingship in 1418 and led a rebellion lasting 10 years, ending in a major victory over the Chinese in 1428. This initiated the Le dynasty, Viet Nam's longest and most stable ruling dynasty, retaining power until 1788.

[4] In Viet Nam, neighboring villagers are literally addressed as older or younger brothers and sisters. Every man who rebelled was engaging his entire family. Vietnamese people do not think of themselves as autonomous units; they do not act for themselves but for their community and nation.

[5] Bronze drums have been found in Vietnamese archeological digs dating back to the Bronze Age before 1,000 BCE. During drought, Vietnamese farmers would beat their drums to notify their beneficent dragon spirit of their need for rain.

[6] In some versions, the golden tortoise appears early to bring Le Loi the sword as well as later to retrieve it.

[7] Vietnamese have practiced ancestor worship since archaic times. Every Vietnamese household has an altar to the ancestors where family members light incense, pray, leave food offerings, and council with the spirits of their departed. Vietnamese families worship their ancestors going back four generations, a full century.

[8] Folk tradition holds that incense sticks are lit in odd numbers, and that three are lit when we have a particular question or need to put to the spirits.

[9] Some versions say that rather than digging Le Loi saw the light in a Banyan tree, climbed it, and found the sword's missing piece.

[10] Some say it was the hilt rather than scabbard. And versions differ as to the exact wording on the sword, with some saying it read, "By the Will of Heaven." In all versions the message seems similiar to the Arthurian prediction of a "once and future king."

[11] The Vietnamese refer to their country as *dat nuoc*, The Land and the Water, demonstrating the essential unity of elements necessary to sustain an agricultural people.

[12] Le Loi's "wise friend" was poet, Confucian, and counselor Nguyen Trai, respected as Viet Nam's greatest mandarin. He advised Le Loi, "It is better to conquer hearts than citadels." Their early friendship is poetic invention.

[13] Vietnamese refer to all their people, Viets and indigenous, as *dong bao*, "children from the same bag." This refers to their common origins as the 100 eggs born in the sack of the dragon and the fairy. To great acclaim, Ho Chi Minh used the phrase in his 1945 address to the Vietnamese people declaring independence.

[14] The original name of Ha Noi is Thang Long, which means Rising or Ascending Dragon. In 1010 King Ly Thai Tho had the vision of the golden dragon rising from a lake, moved his capital to the site, and named it Thang Long. Le Loi's capital was also at Thang Long, but he called it

Dong Kinh, Royal Capital of the East. It was renamed Ha Noi, meaning City in the River Bend, City in the Middle of the River, or City Amidst the Waters, by Emperor Minh Mang when he moved the capital back from Hue in the nineteenth century. Le Loi re-experiencing the vision of the ascending dragon is invention.

In honor of Le Loi's meeting with the golden tortoise, the lake in the center of Ha Noi is named Ho Hoan Kiem, Lake of the Sword Restoration. Giant turtles live in it even now and are occasionally seen, bringing good omen.

In 1963, the dead body of a giant turtle was recovered from the lake. It was over 6 feet long and 3 feet wide and weighed about 500 pounds. Its age was estimated to be 500 years, dating back to the era of the historical Le Loi and his successful decade-long rebellion against Ming occupation. 1963 was a time of American escalation of the war in Viet Nam, which would last another decade. The discovery of this turtle and its connection to the legend of Le Loi was perhaps received as spiritual encouragement to resist the contemporary invaders. You can view the skeleton of this turtle at the Ngoc Son Temple on the lake today. This Jade Mountain Temple rises out of the Sword Restoration Lake and is accessible by an arching bridge. There over the water stands an altar honoring the power of poetry and literature to defend, preserve, and heal. There the tortoise rests.

VI: RIVER OF PEACE

2004

Le Loi freed his country, reshaped its laws and rebuilt its capital. With the aid of divine powers his homeland was secured and restored.

Now the Japanese, French, American and Chinese troops are gone from their land. Next door they ousted the Khmer Rouge and halted Cambodia's genocide. That country too is starting to rebuild.

The wars are over, the sword sheathed—is that not our ultimate wish and vision?

We have never for a single lifetime, never for a span of generations, known a sustained peace. Nor have many of us attained that state of inner peace we long for. We do not know what comes after the killing fields. We may not even know what peace is.

War is always life gone wrong. I wonder, as do many survivors—will I ever cleanse my deep, accumulated pain and grief from old battles and their losses. Can we be free of the anguish at life having gone wrong? How do we meet and talk with others when it was war that first introduced us, war that drenched our minds, relationships, and countries in a poison as deadly to the soul as Agent Orange is to body and land?

I yearn for a peace beyond the sheathing of swords. I return to Viet Nam to seek and learn of this peace.

―――― ❧ ――――

I travel again with Tran Dinh Song. Exactly my age, Song was a university student in Sai Gon while I was one in America. He studied American history, culture and literature but protested our troops on his soil, just as I did. Song spent 7 years in the South Vietnamese air force and after the war another 2 ½ in a re-education camp.

We stand before a large bomb crater made by a thousand pound bomb dropped during the war by an American B-52 to upend jungle and earth. The hole is 10 feet deep and 20 across in the young green jungle sprouting again over the tunnels of Cu Chi.

Conversation in the Jungle

"Look at your earth's torn flesh,
these deep pits and scars,
trees like bloody stumps of arms
held high in surrender.
I stare at this green emptiness
and offer you my endless grief."

"Look at this earthen well
hugging green rainwater.
Look at the carpet of bamboo
sprouting from our earth's deep flesh.
Cleanse this cloud of grief from your eyes
and see."

Long ago Tran Thai Tong taught that we should not merely reflect what is in our minds, but truly see what is before us. How? "Open your eyes and look carefully."

—⁂—

I return to Ho Chi Minh City with a group of American veterans, their siblings and children, and educators and healers who want to add blood and soil to their ideas. My co-leader Steven Leibo declares that a professor's calling is to serve as a public intellectual educating the conscience of the citizenry. We teach history to the next generation, he says, as our best preventive against the human folly that seems to eternally repeat it.

I begin this journey as we have our others.

Meditation at Dawn

Again I greet the dawn, crossing the river's bridge
between walkers, bikers, cyclos, mopeds.
Again I stroll amidst vendors, peddlers, joggers,
tai chi and badminton players.
Xin chao ong! Xin chao ba!
So many greetings my head nods
like an old puppet's on a twisted spring.
To work, to school, factory, or paddy—
Xin chao anh! Xin chao co!
roses, lilies, ducks, pigs, melons to market,
books to read, their language and mine to study.
The early sun cracks the gray sky
until its blue leaks and spreads
like paint, like thick soup, but not like blood.
Here the sky no longer bleeds.

This day begins like every other
except that I am here. A young man, pocked face,
thick hair, smile large and crooked, stops his bike
by my feet as I stoop on his crowded bridge.
"What's that?" He wants to touch my notebook
that he cannot read. His eyes scan my scribbles.
"Viet Nam? *Tut!* Goot!" His smile spreads
as the sun breaks out. Both infect me.
At home I feel lost, but here amidst so many . . .

Every drop in the river creates the river.
Each breath gifts another moment of life.
Every smile, nod, *xin chao*, drips peace.
Perhaps when we have dropped more smiles than bombs,
when our greetings outnumber our bullets,
when our handshakes have rattled the shrapnel
out of our nightmares, perhaps...
Until then may there be many mornings
when I do this simple work,
when I find my place like a grain of rice
in a harvest tossed and winnowed
by the unseen hands of the great emperor.

———— ❈ ————

With a free market and opening society, the Vietnamese are feeding themselves again. But they are in need of enough jobs, services and resources to support their burgeoning population and legions of disabled and orphaned parents and children. They are worried about their youth, many of whom are not interested in politics but have developed a craving for Western goods. Though there are more mopeds and consumer goods on the streets, the countryside remains poor and many from the peasantry still flee to the city to help their families survive.

Massage Girl—2

My mother is dead,
all my brothers and sisters married.
I have no husband,
no education,
no other work.
I do not care that you are married.
I too hope to marry someday.
I will not tell anyone.
But with wars, SARS, chicken flu,
there are few tourists now.
I have no customers for two days
while my old father,
alone in our mountain village,
is hungry and ill.
That is why I offer
to suck or fuck you.
The price you pay
will feed him for two weeks.
Please, sir, do not refuse.
What else can I do?

———— ❈ ————

I travel through the Mekong Delta, viewing the results of *doi moi*, which means renovation. Viet Nam's liberalizing policy was adopted in 1986 to free their hungry land from the depression of economy and spirit resulting from war and Communism. Since land ownership was returned to them, farmers have increased productivity from starvation levels to not only feed their people but to make their country, along with Thailand and the United States, one of the world's foremost rice exporters. Yet they retain traditions and interdependency far older than modern political theories. Each family owns its own land, yet every farmer works every paddy in the village.

Farming

Tending my paddy
my neighbor's bending back
aches as much as mine

My veteran travelers and I sputter in a small, peeling wooden passenger boat through a green world, floating among the lush islands that freckle the Mekong River. We visit with Vietnamese veterans and their families from every faction of the old Southern and Northern armies.

Long-haired Warrior

Mrs. Tien is a Viet Cong veteran, a "long-haired warrior" as the women fighters were called. She enlisted in the VC at ten years old after her school was bombed and destroyed by our American forces.

Amidst dead children
I follow my teacher
into battle

Serving as a courier, she met her future husband, who became a VC unit commander, while fighting the war. Unlike American GIs, the Vietnamese troops were in the war until it was over or they were wounded or killed. Their company commander married them in a simple jungle ceremony.

I speak my vows
to my man and country—
honeymoon ambush

The couple began their family during the war. While fighting and strug-
gling, they had three children.

Nursing babies—
fighting invaders—
war inside and out

Mr. Tien was severely wounded twice. With a joyous laugh he lifts his
shirt to show us his scars. This entire family survived and began a farm
on this Delta island where they still live with their families.

Dragon eyes, mangos,
eels, snails, turtles, grandchildren—
tides in, out, in

Now they welcome us, offering tea, pineapples and red spiked *chum chums*.
They joke and smile with my group of American veteran visitors. They are
especially anxious to hear our vets' stories and offer us their hospitality.

Last time you must leave.
But tonight please dream
on my pillow.

When he first returned in 1985 to this country he had fought, marine
veteran W.D. Ehrhart wondered whether he was one of the boogey-men
parents use here in stories to scare their children. He asked: "When they
tell stories to their children/ of the evil/ that awaits misbehavior/ is it me
they conjure?" We all fear this is so.

The morning after hearing of Mrs. Tien's wartime losses, with funds
we have raised for its building, we dedicate a kindergarten that will serve
two dozen children in one of the poorest Mekong Delta communes.

Kindergarten

> Rice, bamboo, children
> sprouting on this green river
> as long as tides flow

During the war, rice was the symbol of the North and bamboo of the South. Together they show a reunited land. And with children first, these three are the most important components of Vietnamese culture, declaring its fertility, longevity, and life-affirming values.

The Mekong River flows for 2,600 miles through countries that war has finally abandoned. Here the color green is symbolic of peace. In language and world, this green river is simultaneously a river of peace.

In their new bright yellow schoolroom, toes dancing on tile floor, the children recite and sing for us. Then our vets joyously howl, "I've been working on the railroad . . ." Children laugh while parents grin through the windows. We create new memories to supercede the old. We help rebalance the cosmic scales made tipsy by what we took.

—⚬⚬⚬—

We fly to Pleiku in the Central Highlands to revisit sites where several of our veterans served. During our war, Pleiku evolved from red dust crossroads to crowded military support base. Now it has become a busy market town tossed between the old and new, between Vietnamese and minority ethnic group residents and vendors.

On A Pleiku Street

1: Night

> Along the rows of shuttered shops
> the only person I pass and greet
> is a solitary vendor
> sitting behind her metal crate.
> Her magazines are spread

like a fan flowering for ghosts.
A frayed electrical cord
swings from a spider-webbed power line.
She plugs in her tiny TV.
Colors dance in the blackness.
Quiet music melds with my footfalls
and makes her deaf to my greeting
on this empty Highlands street
illuminated by the round full moon.

2: Dawn

Shops and houses yawn and stretch.
"Xin chao! Xin chao! Hello!"
I croak and nod until my neck creaks
to teens on bikes and noisy mopeds,
vendors wending to market with baskets
of pigs and puppies, peppercorns, garlic,
multicolored Montegnaard weavings
and baskets full of baskets.
Behind the dangling electrical cord an old woman,
cone hat nodding, yanks and yanks a rope.
Her bricks float upward through the steaming air
toward the new high storey she is building
on her narrow house from where
she will sip Catecka tea while watching the moon.

Jack was an army chaplain in the Central Highlands during the war. He led services attended by GIs of every religion. He preferred the front because the closer he got to the fighting, the more worshippers he had. "No atheists in the foxhole." He visited the wounded, comforted the despairing and officiated over the dead.

Highlands Church

Between matchstick trees
behind an ammo box altar
he cries to God

Except for army slang Jack did not learn a word of Vietnamese. For the
most part, the only natives he met were prisoners. Looking back, he says,
"I came to a war, not a country." Now he is learning Viet Nam as he learns
the rest of the world. And he declares that he wants to pray the way he
wishes he had in the midst of falling mortars. He had not wanted to
merely repeat empty words and motions for men despairing in hell. He
had wanted an open heart in spite of bloodshed and terror.

—⧟—

Vespers

The moaning wounded,
the crying dead
are growing quiet.

His weary arms droop
from signing the cross
over these lost.

Where mortars whistled
in the long rice grass
now it is only the wind.

Where rifles clicked
chameleons sing
in new green trees.

His hair is gray.
His hymn is of return.

—⧟—

Tam was a child during the war. His father was a driver and interpreter for the Americans. His earliest memory is of falling bombs as his family fled while Viet Cong and GIs fought fiercely for the possession of his Central Highlands village. "Whoever controls these mountains controls Viet Nam," military strategists had said.

Tam was six years old when his village was taken by the North, 3 years before the fall of Sai Gon, "or its liberation," he says. His family moved back. His father was sent to a reeducation camp. Not important enough to imprison for long, he soon returned home. This family was lucky. They only lost their home, livestock, belongings, garden and land, but they all survived. Now Tam guides Americans through the mountains his people control.

Mountain Guide

"Learn their language and be their guide,"
my father said as he grasped the wheel
and I bounced beside him in the green jeep
along poisoned and bomb-pocked roads
while the white giant in the steel hat
ruffled my hair from behind
then dropped sweet candy into my lap
like a gift from the emperor of the sky.
And so I did. And now,
in my own country, in my green home,
so I am.

━━━∞━━━

"Purple mountains' majesty'—here too," I think as we roll north along the bumpy layers of the western mountain range that borders Laos. We pass through villages occupied by minority Jarai and Bahnar people. A loudspeaker blares words our guides do not understand. We pass both remnants of the old Ho Chi Minh Trail; paved sections form part of a new highway while dusty lengths creep over hills and through brush. We seek old outposts, camps, medical bases and battlefields where some of us served.

The Road to Dak To

We leave a green-shadowed valley. The thick tree line opens. We climb a hill crest on which a small stone church perches. This mound was so fiercely contested that after the battle for its possession the local people dubbed it Skull Hill.

> Burning incense
> atop the eye sockets
> of those who died here

Previously the Communist government tried to banish religion. Sometimes, among both the living and the dead, it discriminated against those who had supported the South. Now time and necessity, forgiveness and wisdom fade old animosities.

> Buddhists and Christians—
> separate graveyards then—
> sleeping together now

We stroll through the Highlands dust. One vet complains that her heart turned to stone during the war and remains so yet. Another declares that the things he saw should have made him howl; he wonders at his decades of silence. They touch rocks and search for familiar signs of where they served. They gaze at the dipping and rising landscape, caught in a wrestling match between then and now.

> Singed hills, charred trees,
> my grin that does not feel—
> only old photos

One vet carries a magazine story of an obscure skirmish at Ben Hat. At its scrubby site we greet Montegnaard farmers trudging home. A vet's daughter finds spent bullets in the brush and clutches them like holy relics. During the war GIs called patrols "search and destroy." Now we search and reclaim.

> Bouncing on the bus
> our middle-aged bellies,
> his dripping tears

Our young guide helps our chaplain find his former base. It is on a high hill that casts the guide's home village into shadow. Our chaplain points toward the mountain on which he was stationed, then thrashes through the brush to touch its flanks.

> Our smiling guide
> born as he signed the cross
> over empty boots

Much land is still barren, barely sprouting weeds. Many tree lines are new and low. Veterans and locals remember the bombings and sprayings.

> Tree stumps, shell holes—
> water buffalo plod
> beneath rubber trees

Farmers tend old scars and new growth, transforming wounds into opportunities.

> A million bomb craters—
> cashew plantations,
> fishing ponds

One vet is certain we have arrived at his base. There are no runways or Quonset huts, no choppers flying out or mortars screaming in, to tell him that he has returned.

> All green now—
> only recognizing
> mountains and rain

Old farmers, young villagers watch as we gesticulate and tell stories. They approach respectfully and ask "when were you here last?" "Where are you from?" "How many children do you have?" When we pray, they stoop before us to light our incense, then stand with us in silence.

> Behind every tree
> I feared who I would meet—
> now we talk and talk

Memories return where they happened, and the fear they carried, and a cleansing.

> Where I raced my jeep
> to dodge sniper rounds
> four girls on a scooter

The Vietnamese teach that human beings have seven souls, each one in charge of memory, beauty, will, or another precious trait. When some of our souls leave us we fall ill. In traditional villages, men gather on the roof of a dying neighbor to call his souls back. Our vets declare that they left their souls on these mountain ranges, beside dying friends, fleeing war-fire. We try to aid them the Vietnamese way.

> "Come home!"
> we cry to his soul —
> lightening on the mountain

Among these children of the dragon, I cry thanksgiving and beg help from their father-spirit that brings waters and rules with justice. My uniform in this bright heat has become t-shirts made from their cotton and embroidered with their symbols and colors.

> Emblazoned on my shirt
> green dragon
> rising in my heart

—◦◦◦—

Vietnamese researchers call those who develop new Agent Orange diseases and disabilities "victims of time-delayed violence." Prof. Leibo refers to ongoing damage from old wars as "transgenerational warfare." The sword unsheathes in unexpected places and shocking forms.

We find the site outside Pleiku where an American nurse tended the wounded from all sides in a bustling, blood-soaked field hospital. A small medical clinic stands there today. She is glad it is still a place for healing. But she tells us of the intensive spraying her base endured, of the dead landscape, and of how, later, as a mother, the poisons moved into her. She shows us photos of her children disabled from Agent Orange.

O.R. Nurse

My nipples—your mouth—
perfection! How could I know
my milk—your poison?

· ‹‹‹‹‹ ·

I visit with the woman who previously guided my group through My Lai,
telling us of the loss of her aunt's family during the massacre. She has
devoted her life to witnessing that tragedy. It continues to unfold.

My Lai Guide-2

My husband and I try and try
but each time we plant a child
it rushes away from my womb
to join my ancestors.

My doctor scolds —
too much talk about the war.
But my grandmother, my aunt,
my elder cousins all died here.

Tears for my ancestors,
tears for my children,
tears for the ghosts made of both.
Light incense with me.

———∞∞∞———

Outside Pleiku the mountain erupts from the plain, one end twisting like
a giant neck and head, then leveling off on its green summit. To military
strategists it was the perfect place for lookout posts and landing pads.
American forces surrounded it with the largest military base in the High-
lands. To locals it has always looked like its namesake.

On Dragon Mountain

Bob was a grunt early in the war, his unit dropped into raw jungle to destroy its vegetation, villages, and any opposition. Now he combs the red earth of the old base beneath the mountain.

> Beneath red clay
> grasping roots,
> buried mines

He remembers lobbing shells into a village until it was cinder, crouching in wet foxholes unable to sleep for weeks, not knowing as he pulled their pins if the mines he was setting would explode.

> Stooping in tall grass
> I pick up the old release
> expecting to die

As enemy troops watched from jungle shadows, he learned to endure terror without making a gasp of sound or ripple of movement.

> I twirl green plastic
> between my fingers
> feeling nothing

The mine release once meant death. Now he remembers, watches, waits.

> No blast, no shrapnel—
> a black butterfly—
> breakfast explodes

His head swirls and stomach wretches. A torrent of curses and vomit pours from the mouth of this usually polite, quiet, gentle man. A few of us tend him and nurse the return of feelings buried and frozen under a rigid combat-zone control.

Bad soup morning—
medicine
for my poisoned past

After an hours-long sickness, Bob's eyes shine. He laughs at the spillage
he had secretly held and carried for almost four decades. We rejoice at the
impossible healing that together we prove is, in fact, attainable.

This mine pressure plate
I planted decades ago
opens my guts today

———— ✸ ————

Hue struts beautifully along both banks of the Perfume River. It was an
imperial capital of Viet Nam in medieval times where generations of kings
built a grand, sprawling Imperial City with numerous palaces, residences,
libraries. It was made famous for Americans as the site of a battle con-
sidered to be one of the war's deadliest and recalled in the movie "Full
Metal Jacket." During two wars, first French then American forces com-
bined to destroy 90% of the Imperial City. Soldiers and civilians on every
side were slaughtered here, including old friends from home.

———— ✸ ————

Remembering Willy

Below the scented, twisting river
scarred walls stand in boiling shadow
as gravestone without inscription
to his life and where it ended.

At home above gray Hudson cascades
my sweet wife stoops on hands and knees
to kiss the pine-carpeted earth
above his bones and shattered heart.

Again I visit the Thien Mu Pagoda, home of the Celestial Lady, training school of both the priest who died and the one who lives for peace. I lead my veterans in a prayer and healing circle under a wood-beamed roof occupied by a large statue of Buddha. I know that Buddha is compassionate, but seek to understand how he can be portrayed as fat and happy when there is so much sorrow.

In the Pagoda

"Please, Golden Buddha,
tell me how you smile and laugh
while your children fry?"

"My children at play greet you.
Warblers in my Bo tree sing."

Hue is voluptuous, vibrant, hot, sweet, passionate, refined. Hue blossoms and inspires. Though we drenched it in bombs, its beauty is eternally fertile.

Hue Symphony

I sit behind a hedge of purple morning glories
blaring their trumpet faces to the river.
Below me pink lotuses, whose chorus first sounded
with the budding orange ball of eastern sun,
are closed and resting now. Their long stems
hold high their thick closed buds like horn masters
standing at random proud attention.
From the arbor above, lavender orchids tumble
on vines and chains longer than I am tall.
Their links of soft petals float on a breeze
only they feel that does not cut the steady beat
of blazing heat wrapping tall palms
in silent measures of devoted passion.
Between the flowering vines black bees
longer and thicker than fingers plucking a moon-zither

dance with a quiet buzz that melds with the heat
as they penetrate each blossom
with a promise of honey and sweet life.
Just as I think this symphony of flowers
is complete and interrupt my heated trance
with the tympanic crash of clicking pen,
the final coda floats across this scented river by my side—
a fisherman's flute notes skim the silent ripples
like pebbles of sound flicked by the wrist
of the eternal child emperor who has lived
and played here for as long as the river bends.

With 2½ million dead from the American War alone, tombs in Viet Nam sprout like rice. Many are in large military cemeteries for Northern and Viet Cong dead only; none for the dead of the Southern Army. These cemeteries contain central patriotic statues in socialist realism style accompanied by a motto declaring, "The Motherland Honors Your Sacrifice." Countless other tombs are in small family or village plots where war dead are buried along with ancestors honored for four generations, a full century.

Viet Nam is not only overpopulated with the dead. While the United States still has about 2,000 Missing in Action, Viet Nam has ¼ million. In ancient Vietnamese belief, if a person dies violently or without leaving children to remember them, the soul becomes trapped, wandering in this world and unable to continue its journey toward reincarnation. A wandering soul is called *co hon*. Peasants report seeing and hearing wandering souls gather to lament in jungle valleys and riverbeds.

The 15th day of the seventh lunar month is the Day of Wandering Souls. It is a time, 18th century poet Nguyen Du wrote, when "rain falls like a ceaseless weeping… and pear trees scatter their tears like dew, their dew like tears." The Vietnamese say that the full moon is crying. On this national holiday people tend uncared-for graves all over the country, leaving porridge or bean and lentil cookies for the homeless souls to eat.

Whether lost at sea, on a long journey, or missing in action, when families accept that their loved one is dead but the body will not be recovered, they build a *Ma Gio*, a Windy Tomb. This is an empty tomb that serves as home and altar for the wandering soul to find rest among his relations. My friend Song's family has built two such tombs.

Windy Tomb

Alive our souls
need a house to be home.
Dead our souls
need a tomb for deep rest.
Without a house
we are homeless.
Without a tomb
we wander without return.

My uncle was VC,
his son was ARVN —
North and South,
just like your war.
My uncle was buried
when your tank crushed his tunnel.
My cousin's bones sleep
in a mass grave for both sides.
My family searched
with shovels and spoons
but we could not overturn
the earth and the water.
Finally, finally,
we built windy tombs —
tombs without bodies,
tombs without bones.

Finally, finally,
father and son
sleep together,
rest again.
Once every year
when the moon cries its tears
with rice porridge and cookies
we join in sad feast.

Vietnamese do not ask, "Where are you from?" but "What is your *que huong*?" Que huong is not merely a place. Rather, it is like the *metakuya oyasin* of Native Americans, the entire living matrix of earth, water, animals and plants, people, traditions and relations of which we are each an essential part. Every individual is a grain of rice in the harvest of que huong. The contemporary poet Do Trung Quan has written a poem in praise of this matrix. It has been put to music and is one of Viet Nam's most beloved modern folk songs. As we roll through the countryside, Song sings Do Trung Quan's song:

Que Huong

Que huong is the bundle of sweet star fruit
that you pick every day from the trees.
Que huong is the road that you travel to school
and the same road home carpeted with yellow butterflies.
Que huong is the blue kite
you flew on the hillside in your childhood.
Que huong is the small boat reflected in the water
of the river flowing past your house.
Que huong is the bamboo bridge on which our mothers
return home wearing their conical hats.
Que huong is a full moon night with areca nut flowers
falling outside the windows of your home.

Que huong —everyone has only one
just like everyone has only one mother.
Que huong —forget it
and you will not grow into goodness.

———

Every step we take jogs free old war stories. Many cause pain and confusion. Some we misjudge. Strolling through a village market, veterans recall its old dangers. Some report their grief and terror at seeing children used as human bombs. During the war the children were set with timers or detonators and did not know how they were being used. Que huong helps our struggle to understand.

Song of A Grieving Mother

I love our water buffalo as much as our hut
and our vegetable patch as much as your school.
I love our rice paddy as much as my husband
and my father's tomb as much as my sleeping mat.
I love your father as much as our son.
I love our pig though we must eat him.
I love our star fruit, jackfruit and mangoes.
I love rice whether grass, seed or grain.
I love you, my daughter, as my mother loved me.
No difference between these; this is *que huong*.
And so, my daughter, you and our country
are one and the same, no life without each.
And that is why, with a love more than love,
I dress you in bombs and kiss you as you leave.

DMZ

We travel to the old Demilitarized Zone that once separated North and South. We stand on the 17th parallel, once a place of forbidding violence and terror. I climb on the shell of an American M-44 tank standing as a memorial to the feuding past.

> The open belly
> of the rusting fire dragon
> sprouting pink blossoms

 We travel down the Street Without Joy where in both the French and American Wars thousands of soldiers from every faction slaughtered each other and the civilians without mercy.

> Rubble of a school—
> gray-haired classmates toast and vow
> "friendship forever"

We arrive at the Ben Ha River, the old dividing line between the warring halves of the country. Now the green river flows quietly while a gate marks the bridge crossing old borders.

> Tall guard towers
> staring across the river
> manned by spiders

We cross the river and my vets enter the old North for the first time. As we drive through fields of rice paddies, a combat veteran keeps seeing the peasants he killed. We stop but he cannot get off our bus. I climb back in to help him descend.

> Begging forgiveness
> as his feet first touch the North
> his tears water earth

We travel to Vinh Moc, a fishing village located just north of the DMZ that was flattened by American bombers during the war. Heavily bombed from 1966 on, the people of Vinh Moc built extensive tunnels and lived underground. Vietnamese say US warplanes simply dumped their pay-loads of unused bombs before landing. US sources claim the tunnels were a VC supply route. A Vietnamese survivor wrote:

My childhood—what did I have?
Only the cave that I lie in and the ground that I walk on.

I meet a deaf mute old man who limps as he carries my water bottle for me.

> Our bombs stole his ears —
> speaking what he cannot hear
> his hands beat like wings

We drive to Khe Sanh, deep in the mountains, near the Laotian border and surrounded by the stilt houses of local minority tribes. Khe Sanh was the scene of the brutal siege in 1968 that took thousands of lives on both sides and fooled the American army into distraction while the North se-cretly prepared the Tet Offensive.

We walk the old battlefield in remote mountains that seem indefen-sible. It is not only aging veterans who visit these sites and contemplate war's impact on our unfolding lives and destinies.

> The bunker's sandbags
> where her father ducked mortars
> muffles her sobs

We Americans are held prisoner by war memories drenching our minds. We clutch their pain as our meaning. But with every step we take Viet Nam invites us to transform what we see and how we carry it.

> Rusting plane wreckage—
> standing sentinel
> two dark mountain children

Some vets examine aging weaponry, debate over the presentation of battle history, or flinch before GI dog tags and ID cards in Khe Sanh's small museum. But one leaves the site to play with the local children and gift them with toys and stickers he has carried from America.

> Smiling black eyes
> dawning above
> his purple balloon

We return to Hue. The sun sets behind the Perfume River, staining it with an effervescent rainbow. I stand before a Buddhist altar overlooking the river and contemplate all the changes to the land and the water, their people and ours.

> By falling waters
> a single lotus flower,
> a hand in prayer

———

We end our journey in the City Amid the Waters. We must come home in places we once feared.

In 2010 Ha Noi will be 1,000 years old. She is proud and refined, vibrant and eclectic, conservative and courageous. We visit Hoa Lo Prison, originally built by the French to punish Vietnamese insurgents and later dubbed the "Ha Noi Hilton" when used to hold Americans. We pace its cells not as prisoners but as students and guests. We also visit the Women's Museum, the Temple of Literature, Uncle Ho's Mausoleum. In all of these and in the thronging streets, the spirit of communal determination and willing sacrifice peals out.

Ha Noi grew as a collection of neighborhoods clustered around its citadel. Each neighborhood, called a *phuong*, was a transplanted village where families, friends, trades people and their crafts, customs and practices from the countryside were replicated.

We wander alone or in pairs around the city's many natural lakes and through its crowded market streets. We are welcomed into the embrace of this Viet-French labyrinth of neighborhoods and shops.   I wander the streets of this busy metropolis as I have the red dust villages and river delta communes.

—

Village in the City

One street off the avenue and I am in a village.
Suddenly bikes, mopeds, the buzzing beehive city
are gone. I stroll past poor and narrow rooms
transforming into shops that open onto a crumbling sidewalk.
One woman sweeps with a stiff brush and long sleek hair.
A stooping family cuts and bags melon slices
while their baby sucks and dribbles its green juices.
Old men squat around the bamboo water pipe they share.
The village pond—four water tubs
in which suppers swim in thick schools.
The village garden—sprouting greens and roses
piled, tied, and delivered on bicycles.
I step over the split head of a pig
while a family slices its carcass into bits
to sell before it is claimed by flies or maggots.
Ahead I see thick traffic flowing,
a mechanical river marking the village border.
Though I do not see hazy mountains or emerald rice,
I want to stay in this remnant of countryside.
I stop and stoop on the cracked sidewalk
beside a circle of men sipping dark morning coffee.
The pig's last squeal echoes between low buildings.
Gray clouds open to shower these streets anew.
The men do not seem to notice my round eyes.
Young and old smile, nod, and open their circle.
Together we are drenched in warm rain, aroma and steam.

During the war, in their final days in-country, GIs were called "short." You had survived this long and might make it home; both relief and confusion reigned. But short on this tour means a final day for reflection and thanksgiving, for saying goodbye to friends and sites, seeing what has not yet been seen, completing our yearnings.

Nam is an exuberant young man I befriended during my first journey and have visited ever since. He is a refugee from the impoverished countryside hunger to learn of the world and help his family and other destitute youth.

During his first return journey, Bob posed for photos with a Vietnamese family that adopted him on the steps of the Ho Chi Minh Museum. On this second return, Bob has defused the psychic mines that were set during his combat tour. He exudes a great desire to help this country and other vets rebuild.

I spend my last day with these two dear friends Viet Nam has gifted me. First Bob and I arrange for Nam's further schooling. Then we complete our journey around the Lake of the Sword Restoration and its Jade Pagoda containing the skeleton of the ancient turtle.

Last Day in Ha Noi

1: DRAGON LIGHTS

This is the lake that birthed dragon and city.
Street lights and billboards, burning tips of incense,
the moon pouring white tears
in and out of its old cracked pitcher
tap dance on its black stage by night
or enflame sparkles on its dirty green by day.

Silver bait fish squirm on bamboo fishing poles
and the silver blackens on dead fish
tossed to tree roots. Their eyes are food for ants.
Red coals glow in the tiny braziers of corn and nut vendors.
Lottery ticket and t-shirt sellers squawk and caw and gossip.

What does the dragon think, I wonder,
seeing his egg bag bursting in this carnival of colors,
chaining and blessing with more than eggs can contain?

2: TURTLE BLESSING

"I have seen turtle," Nam smiles, tossing his sleek black hair.
"You must come before Tet. You must wait a long time."

Nam is named for his homeland; both had difficult births.
"You sit and you watch. You wait and you pray.
And if you are lucky . . ."
                    Are you lucky, I wonder,
refugee street vendor, father stooping in village dust,
chickens dead, crops burning, unable to feed his children;
you, eldest son, duty to provide, on these thronging streets
at twelve years old, shining shoes for 200 *dong?*

You answer the question I have only thought.
"I have clothes. I have friends. I read books.
I learn your language. You are my uncle, my *bac.*
Some day I help street children like me."

                              This is luck
on the shore of the lake that swallowed the sword.

3. BUFFALO DREAM

 The vet gone gray rolls again through the paddies,
again lines farmers and buffalo in his sights.
"Too easy," he shakes his head, "I was too good.
They fell with a plop. Hell of a thing to be good at."
His heart releases its vice grip of fear.
His river of tears empties. He sleeps.

A *papasan* sits on his feet in red dust.
His buffalo is dead before him. The old man rocks
and wonders—how will I plow? how feed?
But his children and the village's flock to the beast.
Papa dries his tears, beckons them and carves.
Grief is his weight but his children will eat.

The veteran awakens in the gray between rivers.
He blesses his story. Dawn breaks with his smile.

4: JADE MOUNTAIN TEMPLE

The vet's thick fingers that once stroked his rifle
tiptoe across Nam's scrawny shoulders
as if they were dragonfly feet. Together the two
cross the wooden bridge painted red as revolution,
blood, watermelon. "Melon is best," they laugh.

Before Le Loi's altar, Nam stoops at the flame,
lights an incense bundle and offers it to his guest.
The vet remembers burning tracers and napalm
but does not duck or run. The hot sun lights his head held high.
Inside and out he sees the flame. He kowtows
to the freedom and sacrifice he and Nam share.
Then arm in arm *bac* and *chau* stand before turtle.

The sword is returned to its sheath
and both belong only to God.

———∞———

Months after our "Last day in Ha Noi," Bob said, "our day . . . for me represented the day that all of the horror of the war, all of the nightmares, and dreams of those events that took up so much of my life finally became just part of my story. Not the focus of life any longer, not a time to fear, but just things I can remember as a part of my story.... It was time to return the sword to the turtle. To give it all back to God."

At the end of the wasteland, T.S. Eliot told us, we can find the peace that passes understanding. And where is the end of the wasteland?

The end of the wasteland is beyond the drawing and sheathing of swords, beyond the labeling of friends and enemies, beyond the shifting alliances of politics and history. The end of the wasteland is beyond the fear of self and others that violence engenders and beyond the mines we have set to explode in our souls. It lives where we have shown the courage and done the labor to defuse those mines. It lives on *nui than*, the sacred mountain. It is found on Marble Mountain where, before a Buddhist temple, a simple wooden sign proclaims in both Vietnamese and English:

Hatreds never cease by
hatreds in this world.
By love they cease.
This is an ancient law.

It is restored a little every time Song and I embrace hands across that sign, or veterans of all sides hug or bow before it. And it is found on Lady Black Mountain when Vietnamese monks bless American veterans and family bonds, and when veterans of all sides pray in its pagoda for the souls of those they slew.

When we grieve, honor and replace what we have stolen, when we restore what we have taken, when we receive the forgiveness we cannot give ourselves, when we are helpers and servants in rebalancing the cosmic scales, when everyone becomes human again and everything shows its divinity, then we may discover this peace.

After the Sword

We know the sound of two hands clapping
but what is the sound of no hands clapping?
We know the sound of two swords crossing
but what is the sound of none?

I ponder the mountain of skulls
dressed in gaily-colored rags.
In quest of my answer to what cannot be answered
I receive the laughter of little flowers.

When the waters of Restoration Lake are murky
the tortoise cannot be seen.
Yet still and always, along the dark bottom,
far from lights, calendars, crowds and their ideals,
where only monks' bells, moon eyes and prayers penetrate,
he carries the sword to its home.